WELCOME TO

FROST HEAVES

Other Humor Books by Islandport Press

Huntin' and Fishin' with the Ole Man
by Dave O'Connor

Suddenly, the Cider Didn't Taste So Good and
This Cider Still Tastes Funny
by John Ford

A Moose and a Lobster Walked into a Bar,
down the road a piece, and
John McDonald's Maine Trivia
by John McDonald

Live Free and Eat Pie and
Headin' for the Rhubarb
by Rebecca Rule

Welcome to

Frost Heaves

by

Fred Marple

Islandport Press

Islandport Press

P.O. Box 10

Yarmouth, ME 04096

www.islandportpress.com

books@islandportpress.com

ISBN: 978-1-939017-17-8

Library of Congress Control Number: 2014949217

First edition published May 2015

Publisher: Dean L. Lunt

Cover design by Karen Hoots / Hoots Design

Interior book design by: Michelle Lunt / Islandport Press

Cover image courtesy of the author

This book is dedicated to the good people of Frost Heaves, New Hamphire—or at least, some of the better ones—and the folks in every small New England town, many of which bear a striking resemblance to Frost Heaves.

Contents

Foreword

This is the part of the book that most folks skip over, and with good reason. If you're reading a book, you generally want to get right to it and not sit around while the author hems and haws and winds up to deliver the subject matter. (Have you ever seen a book with a "backword"? I don't think so.)

However, I suppose I can use this space to explain why I'm writing this book, and to introduce you to some basic facts about the town of Frost Heaves. As a member of the Frost Heaves Regional Economic Development council—or, as we call it, FRED—my job is to get people to pay more attention to Frost Heaves, the most underappreciated town in New Hampshire . . . possibly in the whole United States.

A hundred years ago, Frost Heaves was an up-and-coming town. Then it up and went away. I blame this on Thornton Wilder, a writer who came to town in 1938. He said he was writing a play about a quintessential New England village and he wanted to set it in Frost Heaves. He said it would put us on the map.

We said, "No, thanks."

First of all, we weren't sure what *quintessential* meant (but it didn't sound good). Also, we were afraid that too much attention might bring changes to Frost Heaves. Being Yankees, we're opposed to change as a matter of principle.

So Wilder went to another town to write his play, called *Our Town*. Pretty soon, that town began to thrive and Frost Heaves started its long downhill slide. These days, people don't even know how to find Frost Heaves, let alone care what goes on here. Every winter, we put out signs along the road, but that just seems to confuse people all the more.

For the past few years, the good people of Frost Heaves— well, some of the better ones, anyway—have been working hard to put our town back on the map. So far, we have had limited success. (This is government talk for "absolute failure.") But we are soldiering on. This book is my contribution to the effort. I tried to get out of it, but I guess I've used the "I'm too busy working on my sugar packet collection" excuse too many times.

First, a word about our town's name. If you are not from New England, you may not know that frost heaves are bumps in the road that appear every winter—although *bump* may not be a strong-enough word. Some of the heaves make Mount St. Helens look like a minor protuberance.

Scientists say frost heaves are caused by ice forming under the pavement, but we have our own theories. Herb Cullen (more about him later) swears that frost heaves are caused by blackflies hatching beneath the road. (Sounds crazy, I know, but blackflies do appear just about the time the frost heaves go away.) Personally, I think frost heaves are caused by pent-up frustration; by the middle of February, even the *earth* is tired of winter.

The thing about frost heaves is that they tend to sneak up on you. By the time you see one, it's too late. Your head hits the roof of the buggy, your teeth rattle, and words that you probably shouldn't use around the kids get said. On the other hand, frost heaves can be fun, if you know how to handle 'em right. Your stomach goes up and you give a little whoop, kind of like your own little roller-coaster ride.

That's what life is like here in the town of Frost Heaves: There are always bumps in the road—lapses in judgment, decisions that seemed to make sense at the time, unexpected events that shake us up. For some reason, those kinds of things seem to happen in Frost Heaves with some regularity. Maybe it's the people who live here, or maybe there's something in the water. As a lifelong resident of this town, I've heard stories you wouldn't believe (or maybe you would): tales of the unexpected, the unpredictable, and the unlikely. My way of putting Frost Heaves on the map is by sharing a few of them with you.

Of course, I will personally guarantee that these stories are 100 percent true.

Mostly.

—Fred Marple

Welcome to Frost Heaves

The most important place in Frost Heaves, New Hampshire, is the dump. (These days, it's technically the Regional Recycling Center and Transfer Station, but everyone still calls it the dump.) It's only open on Saturday mornings, so if you need to catch up with somebody, you can always count on running into them at the dump. In fact, folks who are running for office generally hang out at the dump because they know they'll meet everyone there. That seems fitting to us, making politicians hang around the dump.

By the way, if you live in the big city, you may not even know what a dump is. You probably put your trash out on the street and wait for the trash fairies to come and take it away to some place like Mexico or Hackensack, New Jersey. But in Frost Heaves, we take care of our own trash, and we're proud of it.

You might think that, as a small town, we don't have the wherewithal for a big recycling program, but we do. Here's how recycling in Frost Heaves works: We take our stuff to the dump, then look around to see if other people have thrown out anything good that we can take home. In fact, a lot of folks come back from the dump with more stuff than they took to the dump. We even have a special little building called the swap shop, where people bring stuff that's too good to throw away.

Every Saturday folks show up early, like sharks circling the bait boat, just waiting for new old stuff to arrive.

Men tend to bring home more stuff from the dump than women. Of course, for every man who comes back from the dump with a perfectly good rake that's only missing a few tines or a three-speed mixer with only one speed, there's a wife standing at the back door tapping her foot and saying, "You ain't bringing *that* in *here*."

But a man can hide a lot of stuff in his garage, stuff that won't be found until they haul him off to the nursing home and his kids go through it and ask, "What was the old man planning to do with *that?*"

Generally speaking, though, people pick up as much stuff at the dump as they leave off, which helps to maintain the delicate balance of junk here in Frost Heaves. For those who need more junk than that, we have a few other options in town.

There's Dingle's Hardware Store, an old-fashioned emporium run by Charlie Dingle. Dingle's isn't like those modern chain hardware stores, which are generally the size of Rhode Island. You could probably fit Charlie's store in the aisle of one of those stores. But Charlie does maintain a supply of hammers and nails for folks who are foolish enough to do their own home improvements, along with some high-quality items such as Chia Pets and glow sticks.

Next to the hardware store is Rick and Rhonda LaFleur's Bait 'n' Beauty Shoppe. It's real convenient. You can get your hair done and pick up some night crawlers at the same time. Right now, they're running a "Shampoo and Shiner" two-for-one special.

The main outlet of commerce in town is the Frost Heaves Market, owned and operated by owner Bernard "Moochie" Mueller. The Market isn't one of them convenience stores—if by *convenient* you mean the ability to get in, get what you need, and get out in less than an hour. At the Market, you're always bound to run into somebody who wants to tell you about their surgery, their trip to Alaska, or the visit they had from their cousin Edna (sometimes all three), so you want to leave plenty of time.

Also, the Market has an extremely limited selection. If you're looking for some fancy imported cheese to impress company, forget it; it's Velveeta or nothing. But the Market does carry all your basic needs: bread, milk, bullets. Recently, they even started renting them DVD things. Of course, there's only two DVDs, and both of them are out right now. One of 'em is a foreign film called *Casablanca* (pronounced "Casser-blanker," for you folks from away). I haven't seen it, but they say it's pretty good.

The Market is where folks go to buy the local paper, the *Frost Heaves Free Shopper*, winner of the Milton R. Furbush Award for squeezing in as many ads with as little news as possible. For actual news, we have three major broadcast outlets in town: our town clerk, Edith Wyer; Leo down at the dump; and the Liars' Club at the Market. If you don't hear it from one of those three sources, it's not happening.

About the Liars' Club: The Market sells coffee, and most of the local guys go there every morning for a cup before they head off to work. We call 'em the Liars' Club because the relationship between their stories and the truth is like the relationship between a fish and a banjo, which is to say distant at best. But if you like stand-up comedy, you should stop by and catch their act. Their favorite topics are Massachusetts, the government, and the car or truck belonging to the last person to walk into the store. I got to warn you, though: Moochie's coffee is stronger than hydrochloric acid—in a pinch, you could use it as paint stripper—and these guys have been drinking it for years, so their humor tends to be pretty acidic too. Most of it isn't fit for public consumption, or I'd repeat it here.

One time, Janice—she's the gal who works behind the counter at the Market—tried to introduce a new line of coffee from some outfit called the Granite State Roastery. She had a whole line of coffee urns lined up like missile silos, with flavors like Blueberry Muffin and Pumpkin Spice. It smelled as sweet as that Yankee Candle place or one of them hippie shops with patchouli oil. You can imagine what the guys in the Club had to say about that. (You'll have to imagine it, because I can't repeat it here.) Needless to say, that stuff didn't last long. These days, the Market is back to selling just regular coffee and one pot of decaf, and you'd better have a note from your doctor to drink the latter, unless you want to get a merciless ribbing from the guys.

The Liars' Club breaks up about eight a.m., when all the fellows head off to work. There's a line in Thornton Wilder's *Our Town* where he says, "I can remember when a dog could go to sleep all day in the middle of Main Street and nothing come along to disturb him." That's still true in Frost Heaves, except at eight a.m. every weekday when the Liars' Club breaks up. Right about that time, the school bus goes by and Ed Whittle, our postmaster, heads out in his station wagon to do his rounds. This is what we call the downtown "rush minute."

4

Cuisine: Not So Haute

We have a few options for dining in Frost Heaves (which I don't necessarily recommend). First, there's the Frost Heaves House of Pizza; in New England, this is what we call ethnic food. Walter Dunton owns the place, and he's always trying out new pizzas to drum up business. My favorite is the New England Baked Bean Pizza. I know, it sounds odd, but it tastes good and keeps you warm on a winter night, too.

If you don't like pizza, you could stop at the Blue Bell Diner, which serves all your basic diner food: meatloaf, spaghetti, turkey, and so on. The diner's motto is "Good Gravy," because everything comes with gravy on it: brown gravy, red gravy, white gravy. It don't matter which you choose, they all taste about the same, which is to say they don't taste like anything at all. (As Yankees, we don't go in for spices too much. If we want to go hog wild, we might throw on some pepper. But from the pepper shaker, not one of those fancy grinder contraptions.) Needless to say, this is not haute cuisine. Mid-haute, at best; maybe even lower haute.

Out on the highway is Wilmer's Family Restaurant, which used to be Wilmer's Dairy. They changed the name back in the '70s in a futile attempt to increase business. You heard of fast food? Well, Wilmer's is the original slow-food restaurant. It doesn't taste any better than fast food; it just takes forever to cook it. That's okay with us, since most people in Frost Heaves aren't going anywhere in a hurry. But if you're planning to eat at Wilmer's and you need to be somewhere else afterwards, you should call ahead so they can start on your meal. Like, a week ahead.

Of course, Wilmer's is more than a restaurant; it's also a shopping destination. They keep a glass case next to the cash register with some classy gifts inside. There's a little plastic cow that you hold by the tail and cream comes out of its mouth. That's quite elegant. They also have a rack with postcards of the local landmarks, including the town office, the post office, and the water department—of course, those are all in the same building, so the selection is kind of limited.

Also out on the highway is Herb Cullen's farm stand. Herb is our local entrepreneur. He's always got some new scheme to attract customers. His latest idea is a new bug zapper he installed, called the Rapper Zapper. It has a neon light that attracts the bugs, then they get caught in the chamber, which plays rap music at 'em until they drop dead—and those that don't wish they had. I tell you, watching that is the highlight of the Frost Heaves social scene on a summer night.

Toward the end of summer, Herb has a "Pick Your Own Zucchini" patch, and in the fall he does his "Bag Your Own Autumn Leaves" special. For $2, you get a brand-new black plastic trash bag and you can fill it with as many leaves as you want. And these are not your ordinary leaves; according to Herb, these are organic, free-range, foliage-quality leaves, nothing but the best. You'd be surprised at how that appeals to people from away (or maybe you wouldn't).

If you want to stay overnight in Frost Heaves, your only real option is the Peabody Inn on Main Street. The Inn was built in 1783 by Ephraim Peabody and has hosted a number of historic figures over the years, including John Adams, Ralph Waldo Emerson, Florence Nightingale, and the apostle Paul, depending on whose stories you believe. (George Washington was going to stay at the Inn, but then he got a look at the inside and changed his mind. There's a plaque just inside the door that reads GEORGE WASHINGTON ALMOST SLEPT HERE.)

These days, the Inn is run by Elwood Peabody, seventh-generation descendant of Ephraim. He's pretty proud of that, for no particular reason that we can see; all he did was descend. Plus, nobody has put any money into the Inn since 1783—the Peabodys are notorious skinflints—and consequently, it's more than a little run-down. The Peabody Inn makes the Addams Family mansion look like a five-star hotel.

The Inn does have a tavern, and that's about the only place in town to get a drink. Lately, Elwood has been trying to expand his market with some new mixed drinks designed especially for older folks. My favorite for the wintertime is Pertussin and Coke. Another invention of his is a Tums dissolved in peppermint schnapps. He calls this the Pepto-Bismarck. And for the really adventurous, he mixes beer, vodka, lemonade, and a shot of Nyquil. He calls this the Hop, Skip, and Go to Bed.

There is one other drinking option in town. If you know who to talk to, you can get some of Bert Woodbury's home-made maple spirits. This stuff is like a cross between honey, rubbing alcohol, and battery acid. I'm not much of a drinking man, but if you put a thimbleful of that in your Moxie, there isn't a germ in the state of New Hampshire that'll stick around for a second dose. A lot of folks in Frost Heaves probably wouldn't make it through the winter without Bert's maple spirits.

Culture, Such as It Is

To be honest, Frost Heaves doesn't have much in the way of culture. Our idea of culture is when Helen Andrews presses the *boom-chicka-boom* button on her electric organ.

We do have a library, the Alvira Thompkins Memorial Library. It's called that because when Alvira passed away, she bequeathed her entire set of Louis L'Amour Western novels to the library, which doubled the size of the collection. The library is open on Tuesday and Thursday afternoons. At other times, you can get the key from Maisie Fernald in the yellow house next door to the library. (Be sure to shut the lights off when you leave.)

There are a couple items of historical interest in town. There's the Cannonball Tree on Main Street, which dates back to the Revolutionary War and has an actual cannonball stuck in it. Just to be clear, the *tree* dates back to the Revolution, but the cannonball's only been there since 1983, the year Millard Tuttle was in charge of firing the town cannon on the Fourth of July. Millard had been celebrating at the tavern a little early, so his aim was off. Fortunately no one got hurt, but we don't let Millard fire the cannon anymore. At the Frost Heaves Market, you can buy a plastic viewer with a picture of the Cannonball Tree in it, though the picture's blurry and it looks kind of like a cruller with a marble stuck in it.

Out on Lazybrook Road, we have one of those historical markers, a brass sign with raised lettering, marking the birthplace of Philbert Twitcham. Philbert was the first person from New Hampshire to be captured by the South during the Civil War, though "captured" doesn't really tell the whole story.

8

Philbert's battalion had been sent down south, and the first night they were camped not too far from the Confederates. That evening, Philbert went to take a leak in the woods, and on the way back, he got lost. (The Twitchams never did have a good sense of direction.) He wandered into the Confederates' camp, but the Rebels didn't even notice him; it was early in the conflict, and neither side had actual uniforms yet. Then Philbert overheard some odd accents and realized what he'd done. He turned around and headed back to his own camp, whistling nonchalantly. Unfortunately, he was whistling "Yankee Doodle."

Philbert spent two months as a prisoner in North Carolina before the Rebels traded him for one of their own. The Union Army discharged him, figuring he was too stupid to be a soldier, and sent him home. We didn't know what to do with him either, so we sent him to the state legislature. He spent the rest of his life there—a few hundred bucks went a lot further back then—and he gave the Veterans Day address every year till he died in 1923.

Frost Heaves does have a few civic organizations.

There's the Loon Lodge, a bunch of old guys whose main activities involve sitting in the lodge out on Lake Mahoosic, drinking beer, and telling lies.

Then there's the Ladies' Loon League. You probably know that loons like to have privacy while they're nesting (I'm talking about the actual birds now, not the lodge members, though they tend to stick to themselves as well). Anyway, the ladies patrol the beach at the town pond and warn people in canoes and kayaks to leave the loons alone. They've done a good job, too. Over the years, they've managed to scare off most of the visitors—including the loons. A few summers ago the loons decided to find a quieter spot, and we haven't seen them since. So the Loon League is kind of a historical group now.

For men, the main civic activity is the volunteer fire department, and they are quite active. At least once a week, the fire alarm goes off and the volunteers rush to the fire station. Then they turn off the alarm and play cards till about nine-thirty. Their wives figured this out a long time ago, but they don't tell the men. They're just as glad to get rid of them for a night.

Spiritual Life

There is only one church in Frost Heaves: the Frost Heaves Community Church. It's a classic, old, white-steepled, clapboard building that sits at the end of Main Street. People sometimes ask what kind of church it is, but we don't know. It used to belong to a denomination, but we lost the records a while back, and now none of the major denominations will own up to us. We thought about contacting some of the second-string players, but it's embarrassing to admit you don't know where you belong, so for now we're on our own.

Being in a small town, the church has to appeal to a wide variety of tastes. It isn't like your big towns, like East Mildew and Milliwillitockset, which can support more than one kind of church, just like they can support a pizza joint *and* a Chinese restaurant. But a small-town church can't afford to specialize. So Reverend Harold Woodstead—he's the pastor—tends to serve a lot of "theological stew." It doesn't challenge the palate, but it's filling.

That's okay with the congregation, most of whom have been around since the last big glacier passed through town. On an average Sunday, when the sun shines in those big old windows and hits all the white heads, the glare is enough to blind you. You can probably guess from this that the Frost Heaves Community Church isn't exactly a hotbed of radical thinking.

The church has suppers every month, and for a lot of folks this is the highlight of their social life. In fact, it pretty much *is* their social life, especially for the senior citizens, who are usually lined up as soon as the door opens at four-thirty. These people make the church supper circuit in all the area towns—they'll have meatballs with the Methodists, then it's lasagna with the Lutherans, then codfish with the Catholics. They have their own newsletter, called "Holy Chow." They do reviews, and they even have their own rating system. We're proud to say that our church is the only one to be awarded the coveted Four Plastic Forks for its meatloaf.

The highlight of the church year is the Snowflake Fair, and every fall the ladies of the church start knitting up a storm, going through quarts of Elmer's glue and jars of glitter, making crafts for the fair. Millie Tuttle (that's Millard's wife) makes those knitted covers for toilet paper rolls that look like swans, or a maybe a Southern belle with a real plastic doll stuck in the middle. Now that's art.

Then there's Avis Thompkins, who specializes in bars of soap decorated with sequins and ribbons. By the time Avis gets done decorating a bar of Camay, you could put it on top of a princess at a coronation. Personally, I prefer the toilet-paper swan. I tried one of them bars of soap once, and I have to say, they're kind of rough on the skin. But you know, that swan could come in handy in an emergency, besides being elegant.

News Nuggets

In response to reader comments, the *Frost Heaves Free Shopper* is pleased to present News Nuggets, a new feature written by your roving reporter, Louise Mitchell. Louise has many years of experience in bringing the news to friends and neighbors. She has an extensive network of contacts, and will be reporting on happenings in the town of Frost Heaves, along with occasional rumors, recipes, and gossip. When not hunting down news stories, Louise enjoys her other role as the lunch lady at Frost Heaves Elementary. "I get some of my best leads from the kids," says Louise. "You'd be surprised. Or maybe you wouldn't."

Myrtle's Day in Court

E very fall, the seniors in Frost Heaves take a bus trip. One
year they went to see *Cats* in Boston, and that was a disaster. They thought they were going to see *cats*—you know, Sia-
mese, Persian, and Abyssinian, strutting around on red carpets
and doing tricks. Instead, what they saw was a bunch of actors
running around in furry costumes, pawing each other and
singing incomprehensible songs. Fred Kimball pretty much
summed it up when he said, "It's no *Oklahoma*."

So this year, the seniors took a foliage trip through Vermont. Don't ask me why people from New Hampshire have to
go to Vermont to see foliage when they have trees right in
their own backyard. Still, the trip would have been fine . . .
except for Myrtle Hathaway.

Myrtle is a kleptomaniac. Everyone in Frost Heaves knows
that. She has been stealing for years; nothing big, mind you—a
can of tuna here, a souvenir ashtray from Saratoga Springs
there. Up at the Frost Heaves Market, they keep a list of Myrtle's plunder and her son Robert settles up every month when
he comes to visit her from Medford.

No one really minds about Myrtle's stealing. They might, if
she were better at it, but you can always tell when she's getting
ready to snitch something because she gets all nervous and

giggly, as if she were stealing a van Gogh and not a can of Snow's corn chowder. In the middle of a visit, she'll suddenly remember something she has to do, and as she bustles out the door you'll notice an odd shape in her tote bag, just like the box of mints you had on the coffee table.

The other reason folks don't mind about Myrtle's habit is that she never keeps the things she steals. She gives 'em away to folks who help her out by shoveling her sidewalk or putting up her storm windows. She does take the labels off so no one knows where the stuff came from. Thanks to Myrtle, every pantry in Frost Heaves has an unlabeled can or two in it, so we figure it all evens out in the end. Still, it is annoying when you open a can of mushrooms to make meatloaf and it turns out to be water chestnuts. What are you going to do then, make Chinese meatloaf?

Anyway, back to the seniors' trip. The highlight of the trip was a stop at the Williston Country Store. That's one of those enormous emporiums that sell old-fashioned Yankee stuff, generally to people from away: long johns, foot balm, maple syrup candy, balsam pillows, and bear stuff—bear mugs, bear pillows, bear toilet seat covers. I swear, they've got more bear junk than there are actual bears in Vermont.

Needless to say, the country store was a minefield for Myrtle. The other ladies—knowing her tendency toward larceny—were a little worried about this, so they took turns escorting her around, like bodyguards, except they were guarding the store and not Myrtle. Myrtle kept up a running commentary about how cute that rooster tea cozy was, and didn't they have a nerve charging so much for penny candy—but you could tell she was just itching to pinch something.

Everything was fine until Louise Mitchell, who was on duty with Myrtle, needed to visit the ladies' room. She went to get Bertha Eldridge to take her place, and by the time Bertha took over, Myrtle had disappeared.

The ladies went on high alert. They even recruited the men, who had plunked themselves on the benches by the door after five minutes of browsing. (Men don't have a lot of stamina when it comes to shopping.) They searched all three floors of the store, from the bargain basement to the furniture department, but it was no good. Myrtle had given them the slip.

Finally, it occurred to someone to look outside. They stepped out the front door just in time to see Myrtle being led away by a police officer from the store next door, a place called the House of Hemp. Apparently, Myrtle had wandered in and pocketed a clay pipe, which she thought was an incense burner. I suppose it was, of a sort.

The seniors tried to explain to the police officer about Myrtle's condition, but it seems the House of Hemp has a strict shoplifting policy that includes a free ride to the district courthouse and a personal consultation with the local judge.

Well, the seniors figured they'd better go along. They all piled into the tour bus—they had to drag Edith Wyer away from the collectible plates, where she was trying to decide whether to buy that year's Mostly Moose plate for her collection—and followed the squad car to the courthouse.

The seniors filed into the courtroom, chattering like blue jays. The judge on duty that day seemed surprised to see that a shoplifter had brought her own cheering squad. He told them to quiet down and asked the police officer for his report.

It was a quick case. Myrtle didn't have anything to say in her defense, and the judge slammed his old wooden gavel down and said, "That'll be a hundred-and-fifty-dollar fine. Pay the cashier."

Well, Myrtle didn't have $150. She didn't have $15. It began to look as if she was going to spend a night in the county jail till her son could come up and bail her out.

Then Helen Andrews said, "I've got ten dollars," and waved the bill at the judge.

"I've got a twenty," Edith said. "But I need some of it." She didn't say why, but everyone knew she still had her eye on that moose plate.

"You take my ten," Helen told her. "Then I'll put the twenty in."

"Can anyone break a fifty?" Jarvis Trombley asked.

This went on for a while, till they managed to raise $142.

"Close enough," the judge said, and slammed his gavel again. He thought about making a little speech about community spirit and how nice it was to see people sticking together when one of them had a need, but he decided he just wanted these people out of his courtroom.

He called Myrtle to the bench and gave her a speech about how a woman of her age should know better, and wasn't she ashamed, and so on. She just hung her head and said, "Yes, sir," looking nervous.

When Myrtle got home, she got another speech, from her son Robert. His speech was "This Has Got to Stop," which is speech number 127 in the *Big Book of Speeches*. It's a speech you generally give to your kids and never expect you'll have to give to your parents when their cheese starts to slide off the cracker.

Myrtle cried and told Robert she was sorry and had
learned her lesson and it would never happen again—all things
he had said to her when he was young, which made him wonder if she was just parroting them back to him, those flimsy
excuses finally coming home to roost. But she sounded as if
she meant it, and maybe this time was different. This time she'd
been caught by strangers and she'd been hauled up before a
judge. Maybe she really had learned her lesson.

"All right, then," he said. "I don't want to hear any more
about this kind of thing."

And for a few minutes, he actually thought that might be
the end of it. Then, as he was leaving, he noticed something on
his mother's mantelpiece that he'd never seen before: an antique
wooden gavel. He looked at his mother, who just giggled.

Needless to say, the seniors won't be going back to Williston this year. They're talking about going to Maine, where
none of them has a criminal record. Least, not so's we know.

Police Log: Suspicious Activity

Chief Spaulding has received several calls lately
about people leaving zucchinis, tomatoes, and other
vegetables on their neighbors' doorsteps when they're
not around. "It's harvest time, and the die-hard gardeners are desperate to unload their surplus produce," says the chief. "If you're throwing a party, I
recommend frisking your guests as they arrive to make
sure they're not trying to sneak cucumbers into the
house."

FRED

The goal of the Frost Heaves Regional Economic Development (FRED) council is to try and bring some progress to Frost Heaves. As I say, we've had limited success, which may have to do with the members of the council. You've probably heard the old saying that a camel is a horse designed by committee. With the FRED council, we'd be lucky to get that close. We'd probably end up with a coffee table.

Take Walter Dunton. I think I told you that he owns the Frost Heaves House of Pizza, where he's always coming up with interesting ideas for pizza. And by "interesting," I mean, "You might want to think twice before you try it."

Anyway, Walter suggested that we should sponsor some kind of town festival. "All the towns around here have festivals," he said, and he's right. You can't drive through New England without stumbling upon a strawberry festival, a pumpkin festival, or a blueberry festival.

The problem is, most of the good festivals have already been taken. And if you're going to have a festival, it should be about something you have a lot of; you don't want to go having a clam festival in the middle of Vermont, for example.

So that's how we came up with the annual Hay Festival. Right away, we realized we had a problem. If you have a strawberry festival, you can serve strawberry shortcake and strawberry ice cream. With a pumpkin festival, you have pumpkin pie and pumpkin muffins. But it turns out there aren't that many recipes that call for hay. Good ones, anyway.

Nevertheless, we had a lot of activities. There was a parade, a hay-tossing contest, and even a hay-carving contest. That was my idea. You may have seen lumberjacks carving tree stumps with a chain saw. I figured, why couldn't you do that with a tightly packed bale of hay—maybe use an electric kitchen knife for the fine details?

It turns out that hay doesn't stick together too well when you go at it with a chain saw. It was like the dust bowl all over again, except with hay instead of dust. And we had a hard time picking a winner, since all the sculptures basically looked like piles of hay. Except for Roy Meeker's, which actually did look a little bit like Ann-Margret. He won first prize.

Then there was the Miss Hay Bale contest, which was fine, mostly. The winner was Jessica Willette, a senior up at our high school, the Frost Heaves Academy. We made a special float for her to ride on in the parade, a royal throne completely made out of hay bales. Jessica looked real pretty up there—at least, at first. Then she started to itch. It's hard to believe she didn't know she was allergic to hay before that. And she probably wishes she hadn't worn that skimpy two-piece bathing suit. Anyway, as I say, she was real pretty till she started to break out.

The highlight of the Hay Festival was supposed to be the Hay Palace, an actual castle made out of bales of hay. We had planned to get hay from all the farmers around town, but we hadn't counted on how high the price of hay would be, or the cheapness of those farmers. Needless to say, we didn't get as much hay as we hoped, and the Hay Palace ended up looking more like a hay garage. You can still see it in the field behind the elementary school, but it's leaning a bit to one side and it's starting to smell sort of moldy, so I wouldn't dawdle if you're interested.

Another person on the FRED council is Edith Wyer, our town clerk. If you know anything about New England, you know that means she has about as much power as the Prime Minister of Russia—maybe more. You don't want to cross Edith if you're planning on staying in town long.

Edith is also the town's information system. She knows everything about everybody who was ever married, buried, baptized, anesthetized, or pulled over for speeding within twenty miles of Frost Heaves. We call her "Telegraph" Wyer. Edith doesn't use newfangled technologies to keep up with what's happening. Hers is an old-fashioned system based on the greatest force known to mankind: gossip.

And the Telegraph is fast with it. One time I decided to do a test. I went to the town office and mentioned to Edith that I had just won the lottery, which was not true. It was just a test rumor. (In times past, we would have called that a lie.)

I hurried home, and by the time I got there, my cousin Frank Marple was pulling in the driveway, saying he'd heard about my good fortune and asking if he could borrow some money. Mind you, Frank doesn't even have a phone. Don't ask me how Edith does it. It confounds the laws of physics, as far as I'm concerned.

Every small town in New England has an Edith, and I figure those master gossips are important to the survival of our nation. They say in the event of a nuclear attack, the first thing to go is your communications—no phone, no radio, nothing. But when all those electronic devices are gone, the Ediths of the world will still be around. I figure if we could connect all those Ediths together and harness the amazing power of gossip, we'd have a communications network that nothing could disrupt.

Anyway, Edith suggested that we needed to do some beautification in Frost Heaves, and you can't argue with that. The last big beautification we had in town was done by the Great Hurricane of 1938. That storm caused a lot of damage in other towns, but Frost Heaves actually looked better afterward. Several long-standing eyesores got relocated, including a hay barn in Earl Hadley's field that had been falling down for years, and Mabel Pillsbury's shed, which we think wound up in the town pond. That's what we call "urban renewal" in Frost Heaves.

Of course, we do have an annual beautification program provided by Mother Nature, and it doesn't cost us a thing. It's called snow. Put a foot of snow on a real dump and it will look like a *Yankee* magazine cover. Of course, that's only a temporary solution, since spring always comes around to expose your dump again.

But where was I? Oh, right, the council. We also have Dave Miller on there. Dave is an engineer and he's a big guy—double-wide, if you know what I mean. He's also our resident technology nut. You know the type: No matter what the problem is, he's sure there's some new technology out there that will take care of it.

At this latest FRED meeting, Dave said, "What we really need is a social networking system, some place where people from town could go to meet and hang out."

"They already do that at the Market," I said.

"Yes, but we need a place online. We need a bigger social media presence."

"Why?"

That question slowed him down a little, but then he said, "Well, because everyone's doing it."

That didn't cut much mustard with me. These days, the list of what everybody is doing is long and not particularly edifying, including "discussing personal bodily functions on cell phones loud enough so that everyone within the area of a football field can hear," and "piercing various parts of their bodies with little pieces of metal." So Dave's reasoning wasn't a big selling point.

I've got my own idea for a social networking system. It's called FaceLook. The way it works is, you stand in front of someone and talk to them. They receive your message through these amazing devices on the sides of their head called "ears," and then they respond to you. This system allows you to communicate back and forth, in real time. This is what we call a "chat."

Needless to say, the council is not going to be developing a new social media presence.

Another member of the FRED council is Herb Cullen. He runs the farm stand out on the highway. Lately, Herb has taken to wearing a toupee, which I can't really describe. (No, wait, I can. If you stop by the Blue Bell Diner, you can order the breakfast special, a 100 percent moose-meat sausage patty on an English muffin. Bud calls it the Moose Muffin. Herb's tou-pee looks as if he was wearing one of those sausage patties on his head. I don't know who he thinks he's fooling.)

Anyway, Herb's idea for bringing Frost Heaves up to speed was to try and get one of them government subsidies. You know how they pay farmers not to grow corn or wheat? That sounded pretty good to us—getting paid not to do something. The problem is, we're already not doing anything. And the only other town we know that gets paid a lot of money for doing nothing is Washington, D.C., and they seem to have that mar-ket sewn up. Still, I suppose we could give it a try. Washington gets billions of dollars to provide waste and inefficiency, and I think we could do the job for just a million or two. All we'd need is one of them voice-mail systems that shuttles you around and never really answers your question, which shouldn't cost too much. Herb said he'd look into that.

Myself, I think if we're going to improve things in Frost Heaves, we need a mascot. Like up in the North Country, they have the moose. Every tourist trap is full of moose stuff—moose signs, moose mugs, moose candy, you name it. I sug-gested this to the group and Herb said, "We don't have any moose around here."

I told him that didn't make no difference. Most of them towns advertising moose don't have any moose within a hun-dred miles. There are plenty of signs that say BRAKE FOR MOOSE, but how often do you actually see any moose?

I've got a theory about that. I think there's really only one moose in the state of New Hampshire, and he's a state employee. I think they shuttle him around and he just puts in appearances here and there. If you have ever seen that moose, he's got the same bored expression as those flag persons out on the highway when they're doing road construction. To me, that's a dead giveaway: that moose is punching a clock. (I'm sorry if I have insulted any flag persons; I didn't mean you personally. I'm sure when you're out there, you are reciting Shakespeare's sonnets to yourself, or thinking about the global economic crisis.)

"If we're going to have a mascot, it ought to be something we actually have around here," Edith said.

"That leaves crows and squirrels," I said. "Maybe woodchucks and skunks—none of which makes a good mascot."

"What about turkeys?" Walter said.

I had to admit—we do have quite a few wild turkeys in Frost Heaves. The thing about those turkeys is, they aren't very smart. If you've ever seen them on the road, they look like a bunch of tourists in a foreign country: "Now, everybody stick together. Where's Elsie? Don't dawdle now. Has anyone seen Howard?"

Also, these turkeys aren't the most attractive creatures on God's green earth. There's a reason no child ever had a stuffed animal called a "teddy turkey."

Finally, they're too scrawny to be any good for eating. These aren't exactly Butterballs we're talking about.

So to sum up, wild turkeys aren't too bright, they aren't attractive, and they're not good for much—which actually makes them the perfect mascot for Frost Heaves. Especially given some of the folks running things around here, though of course I'm not one to name names.

News Nuggets: New Exhibit at the Library

On Monday, the library will open an exhibit of artwork made from dryer lint, by Louise Mitchell. "It takes a lot of skill to make art out of dryer lint," says Louise. "Not to mention a lot of lint."

The exhibit will include Louise's most recent work, *The Signing of the Declaration of Independence*, which is really something to see—although, to be honest, it's hard to tell it from *Washington Crossing the Delaware*, which Louise did last year.

Coming to the Country

New England is famous for its scenic mountains: the Green Mountains, the White Mountains, the Berkshires, the Presidential Ranges. But the only mountain in our neck of the woods is Mount Monadnock, so we're partial to it.

Monadnock is an old Abenaki word that means "mountain that stands alone," and it certainly does. In the town of Frost Heaves, all roads lead to Monadnock. You can be driving in the middle of nowhere, the woods all around you, and then you turn a corner, the road opens up, and there's the mountain, standing proud and alone, like an old relative who's always there, summer and winter, springtime and harvest, always watching out for you.

At any rate, people around here put great store by their view of the mountain. Take the Kesslers, Martin and Sarah. They used to live outside of Boston, but they always dreamed about moving to New Hampshire, buying an old house, and fixing it up. (In the *Big Book of Dreams*, this comes after "Buying an Old Van and Driving It to California" and just before "Remodeling the Kitchen.")

The Kesslers started looking, but the only houses they could afford were listed as "Handyman Special" or "Needs a Little TLC." As you know, realtors have been using those phrases since just after Pompeii got destroyed by Mount Vesuvius. In this area, they always try to cover a property's structural peculiarities by touting its view of Mount Monadnock. "Sure, the sills may be rotted and the roof is swaybacked, but when the sun sets behind the mountain, that red-blue sky will make you forget all that."

Eventually the Kesslers found a nice little place in Frost Heaves, right next to Milt Baker's farm, and it does have a view of the mountain. Of course, you can only see the view in the winter when there aren't any leaves on the trees, and you have to be up in their bedroom, lying on the bed at just the right angle. But a view's a view.

The Kesslers' view is especially nice on a moonlit night. One night last fall, Martin was lying in bed, watching the moon shine down on the bare summit of Mount Monadnock. Sarah was already asleep, and Martin was just drifting off himself when he heard a sound outside the window, like footsteps crunching over dried leaves.

When you're not used to the quiet of the country, there's something creepy about hearing odd noises at night. Martin listened for a moment but he didn't hear anything else, so he decided he'd imagined it.

Then it came again. *Crunch. Crunch.* And now there was no denying it. Someone was prowling around outside the house.

Martin isn't exactly the confrontational type, so he weren't sure what to do. He don't own a gun—heck, he don't even own a baseball bat or even a heavy shoe. The fancy cell phones they brought with them from Massachusetts won't work in Frost Heaves, and the regular phone was downstairs. If he went down those creaky old stairs to call the police, whoever was out there was sure to hear him.

So Martin lay there, thinking about waking Sarah up so she could panic with him, picturing the deranged lunatic who was about to break into their home.

Then he heard another sound. It was a steady stream of liquid hitting the ground. It was unmistakable—the sound of someone taking a leak right outside their bedroom window. And to top it off, the trespasser was drunk; only someone who'd been drinking could pee that long and that loud.

Now Martin was mad. He was darned if he was going to let some drunken intruder violate their property. But the moon was full now, shining in the window like a spotlight. If he stood up to look out the window, he'd be completely exposed. What if the guy had a gun?

He decided not to take any chances. He slid out from under the covers and crawled to the window on his hands and knees. He peeked up over the edge of the window just in time to see the culprit leaving the scene of the crime.

It was a cow, ambling away from the old stone wall that separated Milt Baker's pasture from Martin's property. Just beyond the wall, a large puddle steamed in the moonlight.

Martin felt pretty stupid, but at least no one had seen him. Then he heard a sleepy voice behind him. "What are you doing?"

At times like this, a man has to think fast to protect his dignity.

"You know," he said, "if you kneel in front of this window and peek up over the edge, you get a really nice view of the mountain."

News Nuggets: Wine Tasting at the Market

On Wednesday, the Frost Heaves Market will be doing a wine tasting. "It's the first time we've done this, so I'm hoping folks will turn out," said owner Moochie Mueller. Moochie had hoped to have a variety of wines for folks to sample, but it didn't work out that way. "Basically, we've got Herb Cullen's zucchini wine," he said, noting that it comes in a gallon jug and is an excellent value for drinking, or for removing tarnish from silverware.

The View from Sophie's Bench

The screen in front of the organ at the Frost Heaves Community Church is coming down this week, so Reverend Woodstead is expecting attendance to pick up, at least among the men.

It's not because of the organist. At least, not the church's regular one. Sophie Hamilton is ninety-two, and she's been in the church longer than most of the pews. Sophie never was a jazzy organist to begin with, and she seems to slow down every year. These days, her internal metronome runs at about fifty-five beats a minute, roughly the same as her pulse. She's probably the only organist in New England who can make "I've Got the Joy, Joy, Joy, Joy, Down in My Heart" sound like a funeral dirge.

Dottie McPhee, the choir director, has tried to get Sophie to pick up the tempo, but it doesn't do any good. Sophie always nods and says, "Whatever you say," but there's a spark of defiance behind her sparkly blue eyeglasses, and when she plays again, it's the same speed, or even slower.

If Sophie lives much longer, we're going to have to extend the service to leave time for the sermon. Either that, or find hymns with only one verse. Reverend Woodstead has tried announcing that we're only going to sing the first couple of verses of a hymn, but to Sophie that's an insult, either to her playing or to the hymn writers. She's a hymnbook fundamentalist—she figures if Charles Wesley wrote five verses, he intended all five verses to be sung. So she plays the whole song anyway, dragging the rest of the congregation along like riders on a runaway bus. A very slow runaway bus.

And that goes for any extra verses printed at the bottom of the page. Again, if it was good enough for Isaac Watts, Sophie figures it's good enough for Frost Heaves. Those extra verses are especially a problem at communion. Singing during communion is hard enough anyway, holding a hymnbook while passing plates full of slippery little crackers and trays of communion glasses, all the while trying to stay mindful of your personal trespasses. This process takes some time, so when we get to the end of the hymn we'll start over again and keep going till everyone has got the elements.

But one Sunday, when we got to the end of the regular verses, half the congregation figured we were supposed to sing the extra verse. The other half went back to the first verse. Both groups thought that if they just sang louder, the others would come around to the error of their ways. But neither side was going to give up, which won't surprise you if you know Yankees at all.

To make matters worse, half the congregation is hard of hearing and they're never really sure what we're singing anyway. Reverend Woodstead will announce that we're going to sing "It Is Well with My Soul" and they think he said, "It's a Swell Casserole"—they're all ready to sign up for the potluck supper. Then they'll turn up their hearing aids till they start to screech, and it sounds like a machine shop in there.

Anyway, the result was a hymn sing-off, as if someone had put the song through a blender: "Oh Lord, with all you in our hearts, to Thee forever now. We lift against the holding near and all Thee evermore."

These days, Reverend Woodstead tends to avoid hymns with extra verses, regardless of who's playing the organ. Usually that's Sophie, except for twice a year when she goes to visit her sister in Florida. Then we call in the backup organist, Frank Webber. Frank is a good organist, but he only plays Christmas carols and Broadway show tunes. This is fine during Sophie's Thanksgiving break—it may be a little early to play "O Little Town of Bethlehem," but at least we're in the Christmas ballpark.

It's more of a problem when Sophie takes her spring break. At that point, "God Rest Ye, Merry Gentlemen" would just confuse people. So instead, Frank will play "Great Is Thy Faithfulness," "Be Thou My Vision," and "How Great Thou Art," only he plays them to the tunes of "Seventy-Six Trombones," "Hello, Dolly," and "Diamonds Are a Girl's Best Friend." At the beginning and end of the service he might play "Oh, What a Beautiful Morning" and "I Could Have Danced All Night," but he'll play them real slow, with all the stops pulled out and lots of embellishment, so the congregation thinks they're listening to some lesser-known work by Bach or Mozart. Of course, they also get to feeling they should go out into the vestry and buy a Pepsi or some popcorn.

If Frank's not available to fill in on a Sunday morning, Reverend will call up Maude Wilkins, whose usual gig is

32

playing the organ at the Happy Time roller rink in Maple
Grove. Maude knows hundreds of hymns, but she plays them
all in roller-rink style, so that "In the Garden" sounds like the
opener to a twilight doubleheader at Fenway.

The congregation doesn't mind this, but it makes Reverend
Woodstead a little nervous to see the congregation swinging
and swaying in the pews while singing "The Church's One
Foundation," since the foundation of the Frost Heaves Community Church—some 250 years old, and consisting mostly of
boulders pulled out of Ezekiel Hassinger's cow pasture—is none
too stable as it is.

When it comes to tempo, Maude's problem is the opposite
of Sophie's—she plays every hymn at top speed, which is
roughly twice the speed the hymn writers had in mind. (Imagine Alvin and the Chipmunks performing "Amazing Grace"
and you'll get the idea.)

The congregation has caught on to this, and being Yankees,
they tend to dig in their musical heels and sing slower, trying
bring Maude back to Sophie's tempo. Knowing this, Maude
begins each hymn at breakneck pace, as if she's trying to get an
old car up to speed before climbing a steep hill. It doesn't work.
As soon as the congregation starts singing, Maude's musical
steamroller hits the wall. It's like stirring a stick through molasses.

The only other person in town who plays the organ is
Cindi Buxton, who took over one Sunday when Sophie was
called away to an uncle's funeral. (Given Sophie's age, you had
to wonder how old the uncle was. But no one said anything,
suspecting that Sophie was really just going to the big cross-
stitch convention in Portland that weekend.) Cindi Buxton is

sixteen and she's built like all the Buxton girls, which is to say heavy on top. She showed up for church in a V-neck sweater, a black leather miniskirt, and high heels, which for her was dressed up, I guess.

Cindi played the organ just fine, but several men in the congregation nearly had heart attacks when they saw her out-fit. They hadn't been that excited since Louise Henderson's choir robe caught fire in the great Christmas Conflagration of '87. Thanks to Cindi, the men were wide awake for the sermon that morning, and it wasn't Reverend Woodstead's brilliant oratory that did it.

The week after Cindi's appearance, Millie Tuttle suggested to the church board that we put a folding screen in front of the organ. She said it was so people could focus on the Lord instead of the organ. But everyone knew she was really worried about her husband Millard focusing on Cindi Buxton's thighs, most of which had been plainly visible while she played up at the front of the church. (It was also about that time that Millard decided to get new glasses, which Millie had been nagging him about for years. That just goes to show, the Lord does indeed work in mysterious ways.)

Well, when Sophie came back from the cross-stitch funeral and heard about the organ screen idea, she was fit to be tied. How could the church spend good money—money better spent on helping the poor and needy—on an extravagance like an organ screen? Besides, wasn't that just hiding our light under a bushel? Of course, what really had Sophie's panty hose in a twist was the prospect of not being able to see everything that was going on during the service, and everyone knew it.

The battles lines were drawn. Millie and Sophie are both veteran campaigners when it comes to church disputes, and they each gathered a constituency for their point of view. The pro-screen and anti-screen factions battled it out in the vestry before the service, during the coffee hour afterwards, and at home over the dinner table. Most of the men in the congregation sided with Sophie, on the outside chance that she might get called away and Cindi would make a return engagement. The women were on Millie's side, for the same reason.

The Great Screen Debate could have split the church right down the middle. But then Fred Kimball came up with a compromise that earned him the nickname "the Solomon of Frost Heaves." (At least, among those who don't think of him as the "Neville Chamberlain of Frost Heaves.")

Fred's idea was this: The screen would go up for six months of the year and come down for the other six months. So that's what we do. For half the year, Sophie fumes behind the screen, wondering if she's missing anything. The other half of the year, the men of the church ask after her health, wondering if she gets tired of playing the organ Sunday after Sunday, and when was the last time she saw that sister of hers anyway? What they don't know is that Reverend Woodstead has asked Dottie not to call on Cindi again. Given the ages of those men, it's just too risky—it's a small church and he can't afford to lose anybody. But he hasn't told the men that. Hope is one of the things that keeps people coming back to church, after all.

So now the only argument is about what day the screen goes up or comes down. The opposing sides keep close tabs as to when it's supposed to happen, and people have been known to sneak into the church in the middle of the week to make the changeover exactly six months to the day it last went up or down. That seems petty, I know, but it's a matter of principle. Besides, these are Yankees—in a stubbornness contest with mules, the mules would just give up and go home. So now everybody is unhappy for exactly half the time, and isn't that what democracy is all about?

News Nuggets: Business News

Rhonda LaFleur from the Bait 'n' Beauty Shoppe wishes to announce that she is now a Certified Earwax-ologist, having completed an intensive one-week cor-respondence course from the Earwax Institute of East Irving, Ohio (EIEIO). Rhonda says she can tell from your earwax whether you have a vitamin deficiency, if your kidneys are working properly, and a lot of other things. "This is all very scientific," she says. "It has to do with molecules and enzymes and stuff like that."

Digging Up the News

Halloween's coming up at the end of the month, and up to the Frost Heaves Market, Moochie has Perfectly Good Halloween Candy on sale. (Moochie sells a lot of Perfectly Good products. These are items that are just a little bit past their sell-by date, but they're still perfectly good.) And this candy is a real bargain. 'Course, it's last year's candy, but as I say, it's Perfectly Good.

The day after Halloween is All Saints' Day for our high-church friends. At the Frost Heaves Community Church, we are not high-church. We're more fair-to-middling-church. We don't celebrate All Saints' Day, but we do have what's called a "day of remembrance" to remember loved ones who have gone on before.

Take Esther Fernald. Esther has outlived five husbands, and on the day of remembrance she insists on remembering each and every one of them. It's kinda embarrassing, and a couple of the ladies have tried to suggest that she pick a favorite, or maybe just give us the highlights. But Esther says, no, she has to be fair to all of them. The problem is, a couple of these gentlemen were certified duds, at best. I'm just trying to be honest, even if they were friends of mine.

Speaking of duds, campaign season is in full swing, and the usual cast of characters is running for office. Our state senator, Lester Milfoil, is up for reelection. He's running on his long-standing record of avoiding tough decisions. Lester lives by a motto based on the medical oath, "First, do no harm." Lester's motto is, "First, do nothing."

The Ladies' Guild at the Frost Heaves Community Church has come out with a new edition of the church cookbook, *Frost Heavings*—possibly the worst name for a cookbook in history, but darned if I'm going to be the one to tell them.

Anyway, they asked Helen Andrews to copyedit it, which turned out to be a mistake. Helen just got one of them new iPad things. She's quite proud of it, though she don't actually know how to use it. She didn't realize that the automatic spell checker was on as she was editing the cookbook, and it was substituting words on her. So a few mistakes got into the cookbook, which no one realized until it was printed. I thought I would go through these quickly in case you happen to pick up a copy at the swap shop or a rummage sale.

On page 11, that should be Indian pudding, not onion pudding.

Page 52 has a recipe for diet gingersnaps that calls for a teaspoon of Splenda and not a teaspoon of spleen.

On page 82, in the recipe for broccoli salad, you want to *blanch* the broccoli, not *bleach* it.

The recipe on page 89 is for *Crêpe* Suzette and not . . . well, use your imagination.

Finally—and this is the most important one—Muffy Anderson submitted a salsa recipe, which is kinda exotic for

Frost Heaves. Generally speaking, we are not salsa-type people. Anyway, please be careful—the recipe calls for a *pomegranate*, not a *Pomeranian*. That would be even more exotic, I guess.

Down at the fire department, the ambulance has been in the shop, so the guys have borrowed a hearse from a funeral home over in East Mildew until it is fixed. Makes you think twice about calling in an emergency, I'll tell you.

By the way, you may wonder how I dig up all these stories and news items. We do have newspapers in Frost Heaves, but around here the media is about as popular as auto-body rust: You learn to live with it, but you never actually come to like it. As a result, the selection of papers at the Market is limited—pitiful, some might say.

First, there's the *Frost Heaves Free Shopper*, where what passes for news is notices of the book club's meetings and pictures of the odd vegetables from Millard Tuttle's compost heap. Then there's the *East Mildew Transcript*, which we read every week just for the Police Log, our favorite part of the paper. There's the Boston paper, for those folks who moved up from Massachusetts, so they can remember all the reasons why they left Massachusetts. Finally, there's that national paper, the *National Perspirer*. That's the one with big, bold headlines like TOM CRUISE DISCOVERS CURE FOR CANCER BEFORE BEING ABDUCTED BY ALIENS, or WOMAN GIVES BIRTH TO PUMPKIN THAT LOOKS LIKE ELVIS.

This is probably the most popular paper at the Market. You take Everett Northrup, who comes in every Saturday morning for his weekly six-pack of Moxie and the paper. He used to read the regular paper, but his eyes have been getting worse for about fifteen years, and he refuses to get new glasses no matter

WELCOME TO FROST HEAVES

what his wife Vera says. It had gotten to the point where he was mostly just looking at the pictures in the paper, and he wasn't even too sure what *they* were about.

Then one day he picked up the *Perspirer* and the words jumped right out at him, words like BIGFOOT, ALIENS, and CHOCOLATE-BROCCOLI DIET, good solid words without a lot of nuance to 'em.

Now the only problem is that Everett has started to believe the stuff in that paper, which I don't know much about, except that if I were an alien or a werewolf, I wouldn't waste my time with that paper. I'd go to some responsible party, like *People* magazine or the *Reader's Digest*.

Anyway, since Everett started reading that paper he has been seeing conspiracies behind every fence post. Take Bundy's cows. Bundy runs the garage in town. His real name is Nelson Bundworth, but don't ever call him Nelson if you plan on sticking around for long.

Bundy had bought himself a couple of those fancy, long-haired cows from Scotland. They're supposed to like cold weather, which is a good thing to like if you live in Frost Heaves. Bundy put his new cows in the field beside his barn, but the stone wall around that field is pretty broken-down. At this point, it's more of a suggestion—kinda like a speed limit sign to a Massachusetts driver.

So those cows got into the habit of wandering, and one day Everett Northrup (who lives across the road from Bundy) came running over all out of breath to tell Bundy there was a Bigfoot monster outside his house, and that Bundy'd better come quick and bring his gun, because Everett's old shotgun wasn't going to be enough to bring that sucker down all by itself.

That's when Bundy decided he'd better make a stronger fence to keep his cows from becoming Bigfoot burgers in Everett's yard.

So he got Arthur Bascom to help him dig postholes for the new fence. Let me tell you about Arthur. Arthur came to work for Bundy's father, Nelson Sr., in 1953, when he was fifteen years old. Bundy was only eight at the time, and he thought Arthur was Elvis Presley, Joe DiMaggio, and James Dean all rolled into one, mostly because Arthur chewed Red Man tobacco. (He still does, though there's no truth to the rumor that he's still chewing the same piece he was then; you just never see him change it. Bundy tried chewing tobacco once—only once—but that's another story, which I'll tell you sometime.)

Arthur wasn't any too excited about helping Bundy with the job, since digging postholes is generally about as much fun as watching a presidential debate—maybe less. But Arthur already had most of his wood in, so he didn't have a good excuse, and then Bundy showed him a gas-powered posthole digger he had rented for the job. I don't know if you folks have ever seen one of these contraptions. It looks like a lawn-mower engine with two long handles sticking out on either side, and a big corkscrew coming out of the bottom. It takes two men to operate it, each one holding on to one set of handles. You pull the starter rope, the corkscrew starts to spin around with a noise like a Harley-Davidson, and you push it into the earth. The digger cuts a nice neat hole, as slick as an apple corer going into a ripe McIntosh.

That's the theory anyway. The problem is, Bundy's field is like all the other land around Frost Heaves: It's got more rocks per acre than the Petrified Forest. Every once in a while, the digger would be humming away, the corkscrew churning into the earth like it was Cheez Whiz, when all of a sudden the screw would come up against a rock. Then she'd slow down, strain against the rock, and come to a stop, with a jolt that whipped those handles like a mule kick. This was harder on Arthur than it was on Bundy. Arthur is five-foot-five and weighs 125 pounds.

After a while, the two of them got so they could tell when the digger hit a rock and they'd let go just before it kicked, saving wear and tear on their arm muscles.

By the time the sun started to go down behind the golden maples at the edge of Bundy's field, they had got most of the holes dug. They were getting tired, their hands were numb from the constant vibration of the digger, and they weren't paying as much attention as they should have.

They were digging the very last hole when the digger started to slow down and they knew they were on a rock. But this was not just any rock; this was the Mother of All Rocks. The digger began to grind down, and then several things happened in quick order. First, Bundy let go. Without his weight, when that digger kicked, it tossed Arthur like an old rag. And with nobody holding on, the *bottom* of the digger stopped, but the *top* started spinning around like the blades on a helicopter.

Well now, Bundy was in a pickle. Arthur had landed about ten feet away, knocked out cold. Bundy hollered to the house for his wife Doreen to call 911. Meanwhile, the top of the digger was whipping around like crazy. The only way to stop it was to press a little contact switch on to the spark plug, same as on a lawn mower. The problem was, those handles were whipping around so fast, he couldn't get anywhere near the switch.

He found a big stick and tried to hit the switch without getting whacked by the handles, but he couldn't get close enough. He was beginning to think he'd just have to wait until it ran out of gas.

By now, Arthur was just starting to come to. He lifted his head just in time to see the guys from the fire department pull up in the temporary ambulance, which had the words FERNLEY FUNERAL HOME on the side. Needless to say, this caused a great deal of concern to Arthur, who decided that being conscious wasn't worth the effort at that point, and he passed out again.

So there was Bundy, worried about Arthur, trying to reach the switch on the digger with his stick, not having any luck. And then he heard someone hollering behind him. He turned around to see Everett Northrup barreling across the road with his shotgun aimed at the posthole digger.

"It's a creature from outer space!" Everett yelled. "You won't kill it with that stick! Stand clear while I blast it!"

Everett looked kind of frantic, and Bundy figured it would be foolish to argue with him at that moment—especially since he didn't know what the result of firing a shotgun point-blank at a gasoline engine would be, and didn't want to be too close when he found out.

The result was a noise louder than the backfire from Millard Tuttle's '57 Chevy. An interesting kind of shape was left behind. Bundy took a picture of it, and the people from that newspaper printed it with the caption LOYAL READER ANNIHI-LATES ALIEN.

In the article, they called it an "organo-metallic extraterrestrial life form." Bundy didn't care what they called it, because they paid him $400 for the picture, which was just about enough to pay for the posthole digger.

The *Frost Heaves Free Shopper* did not carry the news because they were too busy covering the Most Beautiful Woodpile contest. But if you want the whole story—complete with more colorful language than I was able to use here—stop by the Market sometime. The guys'll fill you in.

News Nuggets: Pizza Special

It's November, and once again Walter Dunton at the Frost Heaves House of Pizza is offering a specialty pizza just for the season. He advertises it as having three kinds of meat, all the vegetables, extra cheese, and special spices on a homemade crust, at a bargain price. But when you get it, it's just a thin crust with a little bit of sauce on it. He calls it the Campaign Promise Pizza. He says he hopes the politicians get the hint, but he's doubtful.

Shall We Dance

The other day, Dave Miller was coming home from work in Keene and decided just for the heck of it to enter "Frost Heaves" into his GPS, just to see which way it would send him. The GPS cogitated, and calculated, and ruminated . . . and then a little puff of smoke came out of it. I think that was the GPS's way of saying, "You can't get there from here." Just a little warning, in case you're tempted to try it.

So now the only person in Frost Heaves with a GPS is Mickey Edwards, and his isn't even an electronic device. It's the Gloria Positioning System. Gloria is his mother-in-law; she lives with him and his wife Sheila.

The Gloria Positioning System is quite the deal. It tells you where you're going, if there's a better way to get there, and if you're driving too fast. It also gives you a running commentary about everything you're driving past, including a complete history of who lived in every house, why on earth they put a roundabout there of all places, who asked for another drugstore, and that kind of thing.

Gloria—Mrs. Petrie—has been living with Mickey and Sheila since last summer, ever since she got asked to leave her retirement community, for reasons that had to do with a large collection of dentures Gloria was hiding in her dresser, only one set of which actually belonged to her.

It has not been easy on Mickey and Sheila, having her mother with them, and things have been a little tense. Let's just say there has not been a lot of romance in that house for the past few months, if you get my drift. (It's hard to get intimate when your mother-in-law is watching TV in the next room. It's too much like high school.)

Sheila came up with a solution. She decided that she and Mickey needed to find activities they could do together, just by themselves. Right away, Mickey thought of something they could do, but that weren't what she had in mind, and besides, Gloria was in the next room.

A little while later, they went to a wedding reception for Sheila's niece Heather at the American Legion Hall over to East Mildew. The Legion Hall used to be an airplane hangar, but they put a bar at one end of it and a stage at the other and made it into a "function hall." Mostly, the only functions that go on there are beer drinking, lying, and dirty-joke telling. But once in a while there's an anniversary party or a wedding, like that of Heather and her boyfriend Andy, two kids who looked as if they'd accidentally gotten the lead roles in a play they hadn't tried out for.

The band was the Floyd Florian Four, a bunch of old hippies who've been playing together since they were in college, without any noticeable improvement in their abilities. That wasn't the bride and groom's choice, of course. They would have chosen a band with some name like Stewed Tomatoes or The Flaming Idiots, kids whaling away at electric guitars as if they were trying to get back at their parents for some defect in their upbringing. But since the bride and groom didn't have any money and the bride's folks were paying, they got Floyd Florian's band, which played mostly old rock-and-roll standards, the songs they grew up with—"Rock Around the Clock," "Brown-Eyed Girl," "Twist and Shout."

It's hard to call what Frost Heaves folks do "dancing." We just stand there, shaking various parts of our body, looking like we're having some kind of nervous fit, and no one much notices because they're also in convulsions. Good fun, on the whole.

But you can't fake it during a slow dance, when there's another body in your personal space and another set of feet dangerously close to yours. During those numbers, songs like "Blue Velvet" and "Color My World," Sheila and Mickey—for whom two left feet would have been an improvement—sat staring at the cake crumbs on their plates. Meanwhile, Mickey's dad and his uncles waltzed their wives around the dance floor with more grace than you'd expect from guys who have to think for a minute whenever they get up from a sofa.

Sheila was still grousing about that the next day—how they'd blown one of the few evenings they'd had without her mother around. That morning, Sheila happened to be reading the paper, which included a flyer about the new community education classes starting up. These are classes that they offer in the evening at the Frost Heaves Elementary School. A lot of them are just makeup classes in English and math for people who weren't paying attention back in the eighth grade. But they also have classes like Gourmet Cooking for Your Dog, Starting Your Own Road-Paving Business at Home, Brain

Surgery for Beginners, Introduction to Mosquito Killing, and other useful skills like that.

They send out a brochure twice a year with the new courses, and Sheila always likes to look it over, just in case she wants to take up fly-fishing or start a new career in auto-body repair. As she looked over the course offerings in the winter brochure, her eye fell on a listing for Ballroom Dancing for Beginners. The write-up said, "Are you tired of being a wall-flower at dances? Learn how to trip the light fantastic in eight easy sessions."

Needless to say, given their experience at the wedding, that stopped Sheila in her tracks. It was like a sign; the cosmic forces had aligned to say, "This is the one for you, Sheila Edwards."

Sheila had never actually taken an adult ed class, and it was about the last thing Mickey would ever do. The day he walked out of high school was one of the happiest days of his life, and he didn't even like going back to school buildings for town board meetings. But that night, he came home from work and Sheila looked at him and said, "How much do you love me?" When a man hears hear that question from his wife, he just knows the next thing she'll hit him with won't be good.

I guess Mickey loved her enough, because he and Sheila showed up for the first class, along with a bunch of other folks, none of whom looked too comfortable, as if they had acciden-tally wandered into a meeting for followers of the Maharishi Salami Baloney, who was going to try to convert them.

The teachers were Peggy and Leonard LaFontaine from the Happy Feet Dance Studio over in East Mildew. Peggy is a red-headed woman who waves her hands while she talks. Leonard has dark hair slicked back over his head and he wears a snappy suit and pointed shoes. When Mickey saw them, he had the sinking feeling he was taking dance lessons from Lucy and Ricky Ricardo.

The class met in the school cafeteria. On that first night, they started off by dividing the dancers into men and women, one group on each side of the cafeteria, facing each other. Right away, Mickey was back in third-grade gym class and Mrs. Hotaling was making them do square dancing—with girls, no less.

"Now, we gonna start offa with a waltz," Leonard said. (Leonard was born in Maine but he talks with an Italian accent. Go figure.) He showed the men how to do their part while Peggy did the same for the ladies. The women caught on pretty quick, but the men took quite a bit longer; you'd think a bunch of guys who can run while dribbling a basketball could move their feet and count to three at the same time, but no.

Finally, when everyone had learned their parts, Peggy told them to find a partner. Sheila rushed over to Mickey, apparently afraid she'd be chosen as a partner by some unshaven sociopath who wanted to learn to waltz in the elementary school cafeteria.

Leonard turned on a boom box playing a Strauss waltz and they began dancing. I say dancing, even though most of the men looked as if they were trying to stamp out small fires on the living-room rug.

Sheila sighed and said, "I feel just like Fred and Ginger."

Mickey felt more like Fred and Ethel, but he decided not to say anything. Besides, he was busy concentrating on the floor, which had black-and-white square tiles that helped him keep track of where he was supposed to step.

The trouble started when Leonard tried to teach them how to turn. That was just one instruction more than Mickey could handle, plus it messed up his linoleum tracking system. The music started, and now Mickey looked as if he was blocking moves for the Green Bay Packers and dancing to music by John Philip Sousa instead of Johann Strauss. Sheila tried to follow him, but she was also trying to steer him, and that never works. She was like a woman shopping in an unfamiliar supermarket, starting down one aisle, stopping to think, retreating a few steps, changing her mind, then starting down the aisle again.

They were supposed to do four turns and end up back where they'd started. About half the group managed this. One couple bumped into the wall by the boys' bathroom. Mickey and Sheila found themselves dancing through the cafeteria doors and out into the hall, where they got to arguing about whose fault it was. By the time they'd calmed down, they were both too embarrassed to go back in and face everyone, so they just went home.

The next day, Mickey went out and bought a new truck. That's how a lot of men deal with misery: They buy a new vehicle. He explained to Sheila that he needed it to go to the dump with, but the truth is, he was mad about the dance lessons, and also, he knew his mother-in-law Gloria would not ride in it, as she'd need a hoist to get up to the seat. Sheila knew that too, and was not real happy about it, but she figured she couldn't say anything.

Mickey loved his new truck. It was red, the color of a giant cinnamon red hot, with wheel wells on each side big enough to take a bath in. This was a truck that said "Look at me. Am I a hot ticket, or what?"

Mickey works over in Milford, installing water heaters. The first day he had the new truck, he was heading home from work over Temple Mountain, and there was just an inch or two of snow on the road. Coming down the hill, the truck started to spin out. He tapped the brakes the way you're supposed to, but it kept spinning, and all Mickey could do was hang on for the ride. The truck spun completely around until it was headed back to Wilton, which was bad enough, except that he was also in the wrong lane and a tractor trailer was coming down the hill toward him. He managed to get into the right lane with seconds to spare, and just missed getting creamed by that tractor trailer.

Mickey Edwards has not peed his pants since he was three years old, but I tell you, he came pretty close that day. He didn't tell Sheila about what happened, but he decided he needed to work on his winter driving skills. After dinner, he told Sheila he was going out for a while, and she said, "Don't forget, we have dance class tonight."

Mickey grunted and headed over to the parking lot behind the elementary school, the biggest flat area he could find. The lot had been plowed, but there was still a thin layer of snow and ice to make things a little slick.

Mickey started out slow, putting himself into skids and then pulling out. After a while, he was getting pretty good at it, so he started going faster, putting the truck into 360-degree spins. Technically, this wasn't what he'd come for, but it sure was fun.

Right in the center of the parking lot was a pile of snow that the plows had left there. At one point, Mickey put himself

into one of those round-the-world spins and yelled "Yee-hah!"
Then he saw that snowbank coming toward him. A moment
later, the truck rode up onto the pile and stopped. Mickey
gunned the engine, but nothing happened. He was stuck.

He climbed out of the truck and analyzed the situation.
There was his brand-new truck, sitting on top of that snow pile
as if it was on a display stand, all four wheels off the ground. If
he had planned to do this, he probably couldn't have.

He tried pushing it off, but the truck was too heavy. He got
back in and tried rocking it, but it was stuck and stuck good,
right there in the middle of the elementary school parking lot.

He pondered for a minute on what he was supposed to do
now. He could walk to Bundy's Garage and get a tow, but he
knew if he did that, word would get out, and he'd never hear
the end of it.

Just then the town bell rang seven o'clock, and Mickey realized he was going to miss the dance class, and that Sheila would
kill him. He pulled out his cell phone. Generally speaking, we
don't get cell-phone reception in Frost Heaves, but something
about that truck, sitting up on top of that snow pile, made it
into a kind of antenna, and he actually had a good, clear signal.

He called Sheila and told her what was up. She started
laughing, which put him in an even darker mood, but she
couldn't help herself. A woman don't get to laugh at her husband all that often, and when she does, she wants to take
advantage of it.

Mickey told Sheila to come on down to the school with
their other vehicle—which is a little Honda—and bring a rope.
She showed up a few minutes later and they hitched the rope

to the back of the truck and the front of the Honda, but that truck was stuck so good, the Honda couldn't budge it.

Then Mickey got an idea. He told Sheila to get in the truck with him and maybe together they could rock it enough to get off the pile.

First they leaned forward, then back, then forward again. That didn't do much, so they thought they'd try going side to side. They slid all the way to the driver's side, then all the way to the passenger's side, then back. Pretty soon, that truck was rocking from side to side, and sure enough, it began to slide off the snow pile. As it did, the two of them slid to the driver's side and Sheila landed on top of Mickey, the truck sitting there at an angle, the two of them laughing so hard they couldn't move.

They didn't notice that the town cruiser had pulled up behind them until Chief Spaulding tapped on the window. That nearly gave them heart attacks, but after they recovered from the shock, Mickey managed to roll down the window. The chief said, "You know, most people get married so they don't have to do this."

That set Mickey and Sheila off again, and just when they had calmed down, they looked over toward the school building. There, looking out of the cafeteria windows, was the entire adult ed dance class. Their eyes were all wide open, just imagining what had been going on inside that truck.

Mickey and Sheila thought about trying to explain, but they were still laughing too hard. Besides, if they were going to be the subject of gossip, it might as well be something juicy.

They never did go back to dance class, but Sheila said she didn't mind. "At least we learned how to waltz," she said. "Now we can go out dancing whenever we want to."

"Sure, as long as we go to someplace that has black-and-white tiles on the floor," Mickey said, and Sheila had to agree that did limit their options somewhat.

News Nuggets: Swine Flu

A week from this Tuesday, there will be a special meeting up to the town hall about preparing for swine flu. Homer Andrews called the meeting because he is worried about his prize pig, Harriet, who has a cough. We called Harvey Wilcox, the county agent, who says there is no need to panic. "That pig is a big faker," says Harvey. "Pigs are smart, and I think she has figured out that all she has to do is act out of sorts and she'll get all kinds of special attention." Harvey says all Harriet has is whine flu, a disease that usually only afflicts teenagers.

Desperately Seeking Millie

We had a big ice storm this week. Lots of trees came down, and most of the town lost power. Oh, it was something.

The day after the storm dawned bright and clear, and a thick coating of ice sparkled like diamonds on all the downed trees and power lines. There was a strange kind of quiet in the air—the sound of refrigerators not humming, oil burners not firing—a quiet broken only by the occasional rifle-shot crack of a limb breaking under the weight of ice, or someone firing up a chain saw to clear the driveway.

Most folks in Frost Heaves made out pretty well, though there was some excitement to do with Millie Tuttle. Millie and her husband Millard live out on Lazybrook Road, just past the Philbert Twitcham Memorial Marker. Like a lot of folks around here, the Tuttles burn wood, so they weren't too put out by the power outage.

Of course, their pump didn't work, so they didn't have water. But Millard had a two-year supply of Pabst Blue Ribbon beer on hand; always does. It's amazing what you can do with beer if you have to—cook chicken on top of the stove, brush your teeth with it. I suppose you could even flush the toilet with it if you wanted, though Millard couldn't bring himself to do that.

So all told, the Tuttles didn't do too badly. Millie's got one
of them old transistor radios, and she found some batteries for
it. 'Course, there wasn't any real news about the storm to be
had anyway. You'd think with all the other nonsense on the
radio, they might have taken a few minutes to tell us what the
heck was going on. They didn't even use that Emergency
Broadcast System they're always testing, which makes you
wonder what they're saving it for. The Second Coming?

Anyway, after the first day without power, Millie decided
she'd better see how her elderly neighbors were doing. (Millie
is seventy-two, and she worries about the old folks.) She went
to check on Mabel Pillsbury, who is eighty-three and also
burns wood. Mabel goes to bed at seven o'clock, so she wasn't
even sure what all the fuss was about. When Millie came over
to check on her, Mabel basically told her to mind her own
business. Mabel is a true Yankee.

So Millie kept going down the road to check on Jarvis
Trombley. Jarvis is one of those folks who stocked up on supplies at the end of 1999, 'cause he'd heard about that Y2K
problem. Ever since then, he has been getting a ribbing from
the other guys in town about the hundreds of jars of peanut
butter he's got in his cellar.

Millie found Jarvis sitting in front of his fireplace, spreading
peanut butter on crackers and listening to his old Victrola,
which, needless to say, don't need electricity. Jarvis has a collection of old 78 rpm records—the great Irish tenor John
McCormack, George M. Cohan, and a lot more—so Millie sat
down with him and started listening to records and eating peanut butter and crackers.

Meanwhile, up the road in the other direction, that's where Dave and Marie Miller live. They've got little kids, and they were all sleeping in front of the fireplace, cooking beans with Sterno, washing dishes with melted snow. For the first day or two, it was kind of a *Little House on the Prairie* experience. After that, it quickly became a *Gulag Archipelago* experience.

I've told you about Dave Miller, our resident technology nut. After that first day without power, Dave started going through withdrawal—no computer, no cable, no satellite radio. For a little while, he played computer games on his laptop, till the power gave out. Then he fiddled with his cell phone till that died. Then he just wandered around the house, flipping light switches off and on, as if he was praying to the electricity gods, hoping they'd take pity on him and restore the power.

Finally, Dave told his wife Marie he was going to Keene (what we call "the big city") to buy supplies. She knew he was really just going to find a place to check his e-mail and charge his phone, but she didn't say anything. The way he was acting, she was just as glad to get rid of him; he was making the kids nervous.

Dave took off and became part of a mass migration headed toward Keene, which consisted mostly of teenagers. (After two or three days without a cell phone or iPod, the average teenager goes stark raving mad.) They took off like rats deserting a sinking ship—except that in this case, the rats' parents were just as glad to see 'em go.

After Dave left, Marie got to thinking about the Tuttles, and decided maybe she better go and check on 'em. So she bundled up and went on down the road.

She found Millard sitting in front of the woodstove with a ten-day supply of Pabst by his side, and from the look of it, he was already up to day six.

She asked him where Millie was, and Millard said he didn't know—which was the truth. He knew that Millie had gone to check on the neighbors, but he didn't know exactly where she was at that moment.

Well, Marie panicked. She didn't want to worry Millard, so she ran home to call the police—they have one of them old-fashioned phones that don't need electricity—and Chief Spaulding called the fire department, and they called the local K-9 search-and-rescue team.

Within a half-hour, a crowd had gathered outside the Tuttle place, squawking on radios, looking over maps of the area. There must've been a hundred people there—so many people that they didn't notice Millie Tuttle when she came down the road, carrying a couple jars of peanut butter. She asked someone from away what was going on, and he told her some lady was lost and they were getting ready to go out looking for her.

Right away, Millie went in the house and started making coffee for everyone. A few minutes later, she brought out a big thermos and started pouring coffee for the rescue folks, who were just getting ready to head out. She handed a cup to Chief Spaulding and said, "Who is it you're looking for?"

The chief looked at her, a little surprised, and said, "You, Millie."

"Well, I'm right here," Millie said.

"I see that," the chief said.

Needless to say, the search got called off in a hurry. I think it went down in the records as a training exercise.

After the rescue folks had packed up and left, Millie went back in the house. Millard looked up from his chair and said, "What was that all about?"

When you are a woman who has been presumed missing, following the most devastating ice storm in decades, and you find out that your husband sat in his chair through the whole thing, it begins to make you question your commitment to the sanctity of human life.

Millie and Millard eventually patched things up. She decided to forgive him, although he weren't exactly sure what he had done wrong, and isn't that the story of married life?

As I say, in the aftermath of the ice storm, a lot of trees came down. Parts of Frost Heaves looked like a bad haircut. The good news is we got a lot of firewood, and it's the kind of wood we like in New Hampshire: free.

On the downside, some folks discovered they now had a view of Mount Monadnock that they didn't have before. Normally this would be a good thing, except we got this thing called the "view tax," where you have to pay a premium on your property tax if you got a view of Mount Monadnock.

Homer Andrews, who has a big farm north of town, lost a bunch of pine trees that used to block his view of the mountain. When he found out his property taxes were going up as a result, he was fit to be tied. But he came up with a solution to the problem. "I ain't looking," Homer said. "I ain't looked at that mountain in thirty years. I got other things to do around here."

Meanwhile, Herb Cullen turned the tax into a business opportunity. He got in a truckload of little Norway spruces at the farm stand. He called 'em No-View Spruces, and sold the entire truckload out in about half an hour. That's the secret to successful marketing: Know your audience. Especially if they're cheap.

Of course, the problem with the view tax is figuring what constitutes a view. Walter Dunton lives next door to the Buxtons. The Buxtons have several daughters, and every summer they sunbathe out back in them skimpy bathing suits. Does Walter pay for that view? No, sir, he does not. And I guarantee he spends a lot more time looking at that view than Homer does looking at the mountain.

News Nuggets: Holiday House Tour

Christmas is coming, and once again the Ladies' Guild of the Frost Heaves Community Church will sponsor a holiday house tour on Main Street this coming Saturday. The ladies have been very busy decorating their houses. Note: This year you will not actually be able to go *in* the houses, because too many of last year's participants refused to wipe their feet before going through the houses. Once again, a few troublemakers have ruined it for everyone. Now you'll just have to peek in the windows. I hope you non-wipers are happy (you know who you are).

Albert Trombley, Lost and Found

The choir from the Frost Heaves Community Church is getting ready to go Christmas caroling. This year, they are only going along Main Street, and there's a story behind that.

I think I told you about the choir; they are what you'd call "musically challenged." I wouldn't say they're tone-deaf, exactly, but they are certainly tone-hard-of-hearing.

For example, you've got Mavis Thompkins. At one time, Mavis had a lovely singing voice, one that soared like a beautiful bird over the other voices in the choir. These days it's an awful, warbling cry, like an angry seagull crashing through the waves as it comes in for a landing. Dottie McPhee, the choir director, has tried arranging the choir differently, or choosing only certain hymns, but it doesn't matter; Mavis's voice always cuts through. It's like putting vinegar in a drink: It's going to be sour, no matter what else you do to it.

Then there's Ethel Tillinghaust, who couldn't pick the right note out of a police lineup if she had lived next door to it for twenty years.

Finally, you've got Eleanor Bartlett. Eleanor loves to sing, and she's got a nice-enough voice, but she don't see so well, and she don't have a very good memory, so she just makes

WELCOME TO FROST HEAVES

things up to fill in the gaps—which is interesting, if not always doctrinally sound.

The rest of the choir isn't bad, but they're mostly just doing musical damage control. As a result, when the choir goes out Christmas caroling, a lot of folks pretend like they aren't home. To make it worse, last year when they went out, no one in the choir remembered to bring the little booklets with the Christmas carols in them. These are the books they got free because they have ads on the back from the Bagley Insurance Company. They spent a while arguing about whose fault it was, and whether they should go back to the church to get them, but then they decided they'd better just get started. (If Dottie McPhee had been there, she probably would have remembered the booklets, but she had her bowling league's Christmas party that night. And truth be told, she was glad to miss the caroling, because she had a hard enough time corralling that group in the controlled environment of church on a Sunday morning, let alone out of doors. A woman can only take so much.)

At any rate, without the books, none of the folks present could remember more than the first verse to any of the carols, which meant they ran through their repertoire pretty quickly. And what with people pretending not to be home, it only took 'em about a half-hour to do all the houses on Main Street.

They argued about where to go next, and finally Eleanor said, "Why don't we go sing for George MacDonald?"

"Oh, I don't know about that," Mavis said.

George is our town wanderer. He lives in a run-down old place north of town that he inherited from his folks. George's father invented the bread-bag twist tie and made a fortune.

George went to Yale, but then something snapped, and these days he spends his time wandering around town, mumbling about the military industrial complex and reading magazines in the library.

"Why shouldn't we go sing for George?" asked Eleanor. "Jesus said, 'Whatever you did for one of the least of these brothers of mine, you did for me.'"

Well, how's a good churchgoing person supposed to argue with that? So, all eight of them piled into Walter Dunton's old van and headed to the outskirts of Frost Heaves. They drove for a few minutes, arguing the whole time about whether they were going the right way, when Mabel finally said, "We're lost."

"We are not," Walter said. "I know where we're going."

But he didn't. You've heard of the Bridge to Nowhere up in Alaska? In Frost Heaves, we got several roads to nowhere— roads that start out paved, then turn to gravel, then dirt, then they just lose interest altogether.

Walter found himself on one of these roads and figured he'd better turn around. The problem was, there aren't a lot of places to turn around on these back roads. That road kept getting narrower and narrower, till eventually Walter figured he'd better just turn around right in the road.

Wouldn't you know, he got stuck, and couldn't move that van no matter how hard he tried. After a few minutes, he decided he'd better walk back to town to get a tow truck. He left the car running so they wouldn't freeze and headed out.

"We can't sit here with the motor going; we'll asphyxiate," Mavis said.

"Well, if we don't, we'll freeze to death," Ethel said.

So they argued about that for a while, but then the problem solved itself. The van ran out of gas.

"Now what are we going to do?" Eleanor said.

"I don't know about you," Joe Hoffman said, "but I got to take a leak."

Joe headed off into the woods, and he hadn't got too far when he saw an old hunting shack leaning against a big old maple out there in the middle of the woods. He peeked in the windows and there was an old woodstove and some kindling in a basket. It didn't look as if anyone had been there in a long time, but he figured they could wait in there and keep warm while they were waiting for Walter.

Joe took care of his business and went back to tell the others. A little while later they were all sitting in the shack, enjoying the warmth of the stove; it was actually quite cozy.

Then it started to snow.

"Well, here we are," Eleanor said. "We might as well make the best of it. Let's sing."

So they did. They sang Christmas carols, and when they ran through them, they sang old love songs, and silly songs they remembered from when they were youngsters—"Don't Fence Me In," "Minnie the Moocher," and "Mairzy Doats." Then they'd go back and sing the Christmas carols again. They weren't trying to impress anyone, because there was no one else around. They were just doing it for the love of singing, and for once, they actually sounded pretty good.

They hadn't sounded that good since they'd lost Mary Trombley, earlier that year. Mary had been in the choir for forty years, and in a way, she was its heart and soul. Then she passed away, and the choir had never really been the same after that.

They weren't the only ones. Mary's husband Albert hadn't been the same either. Albert is a quiet guy, and he was always in Mary's shadow, especially at Christmastime.

Christmas was Mary's thing. Every year, she decorated the house like it was the Magic Kingdom. She threw parties. She collected toys for poor kids. She made cookies for the mailman, the folks at the dump, and shut-ins. I tell you, she was the queen of Christmas.

To be honest, it drove Albert crazy. For the entire month of December, he felt like a visitor in his own house. He couldn't use the towels in the bathroom—she always put out little guest towels with pictures of Santa and Mrs. Claus on them—so he learned how to dry his hands on the window curtains. He couldn't eat a cookie without being told it was for some party. She would put away his favorite coffee mug and make him use one with a Christmas tree that lit up when you poured hot water into it. And she went around the house all day long, humming "Silent Night," which was her favorite carol.

This went on for thirty years. To Albert, it began to feel like he'd no more than put the Christmas decorations up in the attic, and a week later he was taking them down again.

Then Mary passed away, and when Christmas rolled around, Albert didn't do any of those things. He just rumbled around that big old house by himself. He's got two daughters, one in California and one in Texas, and they wanted him to come spend Christmas with them, but he just made up excuses why he couldn't go.

So there Albert was, the week before Christmas, watching
It's a Wonderful Life on TV and drinking a glass of Moxie with a
shot of Bert Woodbury's homemade maple spirits in it. He got
to feeling sentimental, and thought maybe he *would* put up a
Christmas tree (which isn't the stupidest thing anyone's ever
done under the influence of Bert's maple spirits).

He found his little hatchet and headed out in the woods
behind the house. It was a cold evening, and the sun was heading
low into the trees. There weren't any good trees to be seen, so he
kept going deeper into the woods. After a while, the wind started
to pick up, and he figured he'd better make up his mind soon.

Then he saw it—the perfect tree, just about chest-high, nice
and full all around. He pushed aside the bottom branches and
leaned over with the hatchet. Then his glasses fell off. Without
his glasses, Albert is practically blind. He took a step and heard a
sickening crunch that told him he'd just destroyed his glasses.

At that point, he figured he'd better just head on home.
That was the end of the Christmas tree hunt. The problem was,
without his glasses, he didn't know where home was. He
turned and started wandering in what he thought was the general direction of home, but he pretty quick realized he had no
idea if he was headed home or just getting more and more lost.

After a few minutes of this, Albert stumbled over a big old
log. He thought it might be time to sit down and think things
over, and this was as good a place as any to do it.

As he sat there, he got to thinking about being lost. He
thought about the Wise Men, traveling all the way from Baby-
lon to Bethlehem, not exactly sure where they were going. He
thought about a young Jewish couple, expecting their first baby,

traipsing around a strange city trying to find a place to spend the night. He thought about himself, being lost out there in the woods. And for the first time since Mary had passed away, he realized how totally and completely lost he was without her.

The wind died down a bit, and it started to snow—real pretty, like Hollywood snow—so light and fluffy, it almost doesn't seem real. After a while, he wasn't feeling so cold anymore. Then he realized that wasn't necessarily a good sign. He knew he'd better get up and start walking, because if he just sat there, he was going to freeze to death.

Then he thought, *Why not?* Why not just sit here? All that would happen was that he'd be able to see Mary again.

So that's what Albert did. He just sat there. And after a few minutes, sure enough, he started to hear angels singing. And as it happens, they were singing Mary's favorite Christmas carol.

Silent night, holy night.
All is calm, all is bright.

He was a little surprised that the angels only knew the first verse to "Silent Night"—you'd think that if anyone should know all the verses, it would be a bunch of angels. He was even more surprised when they started singing "Does Your Chewing Gum Lose its Flavor on the Bedpost Overnight?" He began to think maybe Heaven was going to be a more interesting place than he'd expected.

He figured he'd better see what kind of angels these were, so he got up and followed the sound of the singing. A couple minutes later, he came to a little hunting shack. Inside the shack, Mabel had just started to lead the group in singing "Nearer My God to Thee." Albert threw open the door, which almost sent Mabel very near to God indeed. When you're sitting in a shack on a snowy night and you suddenly see someone standing in the doorway, covered in snow, with an ax in his hand, your mind kinda naturally goes to backwoods psychopath, not Santa Claus.

But eventually they got things straightened out, and Albert and the choir did find their way back home.

Anyway, that explains why the choir's only going to be caroling on Main Street this year. If they get done early, they may go over to Albert's house. He's got it all done up for Christmas. He hauled all of Mary's decorations out, and the place looks real nice. If you want, you could stop by and say hi. But I'd knock before you go in.

News Nuggets: New Year's Dinner

Make your plans now to spend New Year's Eve at the Blue Bell Diner, featuring the Gravy Jamboree, a four-course meal that includes crackers with fine, aged cheese sauce; choice of meatloaf, chicken, or spaghetti, with sauce or gravy; salad with Bud's special creamy bean dressing (left over from Bud's ill-fated foray into Mexican food); and dessert, a choice of zucchini ice cream or apple pie with fine, aged cheese sauce. Angus McPhee will provide musical accompaniment, performing all your favorite tunes on the bagpipe. You haven't lived until you've heard "Smoke on the Water" played on a bagpipe.

No Business Like Snow Business

This year, the annual Frost Heaves winter carnival kicked off down at the town pond with Mavis Thompkins singing the national anthem over the loudspeaker. I've told you about Mavis; she has a voice that'll remove stubborn stains from laundry. By the time she hit that high part on "the rockets' red glare," most of the dogs in town were hiding in the cellar. And by the time she dragged Old Glory over the finish line, it's amazing there were any stars left on it.

Right after Mavis sang came the start of the ice-fishing contest. The guys all stood around their fishing holes, watching the lines, but they weren't getting any bites, nary a one. It took them a while to figure out that Mavis's singing had scared all the fish away. Needless to say, this ruined the contest, although it did give Herb Cullen an idea. He's thinking of taking Mavis around to some of them lakes that are being overrun by invasive species, like these Asian carp you've heard about. Herb figures it's an all-natural way to deal with the problem. Of course, we don't know if there would be side effects on the plant life; that still needs to be studied.

Another winter carnival event was the town-wide snow sculpture contest. The winner of the contest was Bert Woodbury, with his highly detailed sculpture of a '67 Chevy truck.

Unfortunately, Bert was stripped of the prize when we found out that his sculpture actually *was* his '67 Chevy, parked at the end of his driveway. The town plow had covered it up, so he had just packed the snow around it.

Millard Tuttle won the People's Choice Award for his sculpture of a beer cooler, complete with actual beer inside. That's probably because the people voting were mostly the ice-fishermen, who had a lot of time on their hands, as it happens.

There was the free-for-all sled race on Swedes Hill, with every kind of contraption you can think of: flying saucers, toboggans, and plenty of newfangled sleds. But the winner of the contest, believe it or not, was Bob Cooper, who actually road a shovel down the hill. Remember the opening scene of *It's a Wonderful Life*, where the kids are riding shovels down the hill? You put your bottom on the shovel with the handle pointing forward, lean back, and let go.

The problem came when Bob got to the bottom of the hill and needed to stop so he wouldn't slam into the side of the elementary school. He wasn't sure how to stop, and he hadn't really thought this out beforehand, so he just grabbed the handle. He did stop, but let's just say it's a good thing Bob already has all the kids he wants.

That evening, over at the town hall, we had one of them silent auction things. It didn't work out too well. Herb Cullen would hold something up, and we all just sat there looking at him, wondering if we were supposed to be using mental telegraphy or something. Eventually we just went back to the old way of doing it, with actual words. I don't know why them silent auctions are so popular.

70

But the highlight of the carnival was the synchronized snowblowing event. There's a group of guys in town—they call themselves the Snow Men—and they had been practicing all winter long. There's about a dozen men in the squad.

Vern Mullens headed up the group, an old bachelor from town, the kind of guy who's kinda crusty on the outside, but inside, just the nicest guy you'd ever want to know, always doing for folks and helping 'em out. I can't tell you how many rides he has given folks over the years, and would never take a cent for it. One time he gave a ride to Jenny MacDonald— she's a single mom from town—when she had to take one of her kids up to Concord to see a specialist. After Vern dropped them off at home, he found a $20 bill on the backseat, and he knew Jenny had left it, and he knew she'd never take it back.

So the next time he saw her, sitting with the kids at the counter of the Blue Bell Diner, he sat down next to her to say hello, and when she got home she found a $20 bill tucked in her coat pocket. Well, that turned into a kind of game between the two of them. Vern would open his front door to find the $20 bill sticking out from under the doormat. Then she'd find it in a flowerpot on her stoop. Oh, they got real creative. One time, he tied it in a ribbon and put it around the neck of her little Sheltie, like he was a cross between a Saint Bernard and an ATM. Quite a sense of humor, that Vern.

Anyway, the synchronized snowblower squad was his idea. He got the troop together and started teaching them this com- plex routine set to music, like "Cold as Ice" and "Snowbound." Vern used his fancy, competition snowblower, "Old Faceful," instead of his everyday blower.

But then one of the guys moved away, and another sold his snowblower, so Vern put up a note at the diner, looking for a couple volunteers to join the group.

The next Saturday, the guys were standing around the field behind the elementary school where they practice, and they heard the sound of a snowblower coming down the street. They looked up, and it was none other than Jenny MacDonald, steering a beat-up old Toro blower down the sidewalk.

The guys were all watching and Vern said, "Jenny, what's up?"

"Heard you needed help," Jenny said. "Thought I'd join in."

Well, they had never had a woman in the group before. Vern didn't want to hurt her feelings. He said, "You know, this ain't ordinary snowblowing."

"I know that," Jenny said.

"It's pretty complicated," Vern said. "And we don't have much time till the winter carnival."

"I can do it," she said.

Ed Whittle decided to jump in at this point. "You'll have to pass the qualification test," he said.

Needless to say, none of the guys had ever passed any qualification test to be on the squad other than to be upright and breathing.

"Fine," Jenny said.

So Ed put her through a few simple paces, and she did 'em fine. Then he gave her some harder moves, and she did them too. By now, the guys were all looking at each other with raised eyebrows, thinking, "She's good."

What these guys didn't realize was that, being a single mom, Jenny was used to steering a grocery cart around them skinny aisles of the MegaMart, one kid in the cart and another one in a stroller. This was nothing for her.

Ed was still looking for a way out of this, so he asked her a few questions about snowblower maintenance and such, all of which she answered fine. Then he gave her a trick question. He asked her to explain Pinchley's Paradox.

Jenny looked him in the eye and said, "Pinchley's Paradox was formulated by Hubert Pinchley, an amateur mathematician and snowblower enthusiast from East Turnbuckle, Vermont. It states that the more snowblowers you run, the faster you can clear a given area. But with each added snowblower, the greater the chance that two or more snowblowers will toss snow on each other. The paradox involves figuring out the ideal number of blowers and the best pattern to clear an area in the shortest possible time. No one has ever solved Pinchley's Paradox."

After that, there weren't much the guys could say. She had passed the test with flying colors, and Vern made her a member of the group. For the next several weeks, they all worked hard, learning the routine Vern had come up with, and they were looking really sharp.

Then, the week before the carnival, Vern was out snow-blowing his driveway when he felt a kinda funny feeling in his chest. He went inside and called Doc Shepherd, who came right over. The not-too-long and short of it was that Vern had had a minor heart attack, and there was no way Doc Shepherd was going to let him lead the synchronized snowblower squad at the winter carnival.

Vern thought long and hard, and he realized that the only person who could really take his place was Jenny. He knew it was probably going to tick the other guys off, but he always believed in getting the best man for the job, even if that man was a woman.

He called her up and asked her to do it, and he told her she could even use his special, competition blower. Jenny thought about it and told him she'd do it, but only if she could use her own machine. Vern said okay.

The day of the carnival came, and everyone in town was gathered on the hillside around the town pond. The guys had roped off an area of the ice, and there was a nice fresh layer of snow there.

Vern was watching as the music began and the squad started up. Right away, he could see they were in trouble. They weren't doing the routine he'd come up with at all. Panic-stricken, all he could do was stare. But then, as he watched, he realized there was an odd kind of sense to the pattern they were doing. And then he realized what was happening.

Jenny was solving Pinchley's Paradox right before their eyes. In three minutes the Snow Men, led by Jenny MacDonald, had cleared the entire area, using a pattern that has since become known as the Spinning Jenny. The crowd erupted in cheers. It was the most thrilling thing they had ever seen.

It was maybe a little too thrilling for Vern. That night, he had another heart attack, and this was the big one, the one that punched his ticket and sent him on to his reward.

Needless to say, Jenny was devastated. She was really going to miss that old coot.

On Tuesday, she went to the visiting hours at Fernley Funeral Home, knelt at the casket, and said a prayer, bawling her eyes out. Eventually, she pulled herself together, and by the time she stepped away from the casket, she seemed okay. She was even smiling a little through the tears.

The folks who stepped up to the casket after Jenny were a little surprised to see a $20 bill tucked into the lining, next to Vern. But they just figured it's a small town, and folks believe in paying their debts, no matter how late.

News Nuggets: Back to School

On Monday, January 5, the kids will all be going back to school after the Christmas holidays. This has been designated as "Parental Emancipation Day" by several of the mothers of small children, who will be gathering at the Peabody Inn tavern to discuss parenting issues while enjoying their favorite adult beverages. Husbands are instructed to heat up some hot dogs if the ladies are not home in time for dinner.

Remote Possibilities

The guys at the Market were griping about winter one day, arguing about what possible good it could be. Walter gave his opinion that it was designed to keep down the pests—flies, mosquitoes, summer people. Don't get me wrong; we like summer people. From June to August, they provide about the only real income we have. But we feel about 'em the same way we feel about relatives—happy to see 'em come, happier to see 'em go. (By the way, if you happen to be a summer person, please don't take offense. There are plenty of things we aren't even happy to see coming, including blackflies and politicians.)

The big problem with winter is it complicates everything. You take Agnes Letourneau; she lives on Main Street, just down from the library. She likes to walk to the library to get her Louis L'Amour Western novels, but in the winter she can't, what with all the snow on the sidewalks, and it isn't safe to walk in the street.

Agnes called up the town office and complained about the sidewalks. Rudy Zimmerman was on duty in the office that day, and he tried to explain to Agnes that there wasn't any money in the budget for shoveling sidewalks. Agnes hung up, none too pleased, and figured she'd just have to settle for reading *Outlaw Riders of the Lost Broken Creek Canyon Trail* one more time.

After he hung up, Rudy got to feeling bad about Agnes. He thought about trying to get some volunteers together to shovel her sidewalk, but Agnes tends to be picky, and no one needs constructive criticism when they're trying to do a good deed. Besides, Rudy doesn't even like clearing his own driveway. He lives on Swedes Hill at the end of Main Street, and has a long driveway. He's too cheap to pay someone to plow it, so he bought a snowblower, and he don't even like using that. Jostling and tugging that snowblower around bothers his bad back. The first storm we had after Christmas, clearing the driveway took Rudy a couple of hours. He don't like being outside anyway; he'd rather be in his workshop, tinkering with something.

As it happens, Rudy's son and his family were visiting at the time, and his grandson was driving him crazy with a remote-control truck he had gotten for Christmas, racing it all over the house, banging into things. But that truck gave Rudy an idea.

After the kids left, he went to Toy-a-Rama over to Keene and bought a remote-control truck just like his grandson's. He brought it home, took it apart, and hooked it up to the snow-blower, along with one of them remote starters.

Rudy couldn't wait for the next storm so's he could try out his automatic snowblower, and he finally got his chance a few weeks ago. We had about six inches of snow, and I tell you, that gizmo worked slick. Rudy sat inside, looking out his big picture window, nice and toasty, steering his remote-controlled snowblower as it puttered down the driveway, doing its thing.

What Rudy hadn't figured on was the range of that remote-control device—which, according to the box the truck came in, was about fifty feet. As it happens, Rudy's driveway is fifty-one

feet long. So when the snowblower got to the end of the driveway and Rudy tried to turn it around, it just kept going.

Rudy started hollering, but hollering at a machine rarely
does any good, as you know if you've ever tried it. He threw
on his boots and jacket and ran out of the house after it. At the
top of the driveway he hit a patch of ice and went down hard
on his keister. Of course, that sent his back into a spasm, and he
couldn't move.

So there Rudy lay, staring up at the sky, snow falling on him,
his snowblower chugging down Swedes Hill Road toward town.

Upstairs in the bedroom, Rudy's wife Nadine heard the
commotion and looked out the window. She saw him lying in
the driveway and said, "Oh, now he's done it; he's gone and
had a heart attack." She grabbed the phone and called 911.

Within minutes, the guys from the fire station were on
their way to Rudy's house. As they raced up the hill, they
passed a snowblower headed toward town all by itself. They
wondered about that, but figured they didn't have time to
worry about it. When someone's having a heart attack, those
first few minutes are crucial.

They showed up at Rudy's house and there Rudy was, flat
on his back, arguing with Nadine and hollering about the
snowblower. She was hollering back at him, telling him he was
hallucinating, and that if he went and died, she would kill him.

Meanwhile, down on Main Street, Agnes Letourneau was
doing laundry in the basement when she heard a racket outside.
She came upstairs a few minutes later and saw that someone
had cleared the sidewalk in front of the house. She went out to
check their work and realized they'd cleared all the way to the

library. In fact, they had cleared the entire length of Main Street and then some, as far as the town pond. They'd even cleared a path across the pond and into the woods on the other side.

She wasn't sure why they'd gone to all that trouble—she rarely went as far as the pond, and didn't plan to go out on the ice anytime soon—but she was tickled pink nevertheless. It restored her faith in government, which had been taking a beating lately.

That was a while ago now. Rudy has recovered from his fall, and he's thinking about his next project. He's got about three feet of snow on his roof, and it's going to be a backbreaking job to get it off with a roof rake. He has been wondering if there might be some way to get a snowblower up there. He doesn't have one right now, so he's thinking of something that involves a shop vac and a long hose. Nadine, she just keeps counting the days till winter is over.

Meeting Notes: Frost Heaves Regional Economic Development Council

At the February 10 meeting of FRED, Walter Dunton proposed that the town begin an "Adopt a Heave" program. The idea would be to put a sign by each heave, saying, "This frost heave brought to you by the Blue Bell Diner," and so on. Walter figures we might be able to make enough money to actually fix some of the heaves. The rest of the council said this was probably the dumbest idea they'd ever heard, but decided to give it a try anyway.

Burnt Offerings

As I've mentioned, the Frost Heaves Community Church isn't what you'd call "high-church." Folks around here don't go in for show. At Easter, the choir wears maroon robes and the altar has a single white candle on it—but that's about as close to pageantry as we get.

Every once in a while, though, Pastor Woodstead gets to thinking he needs to do something different to shake the congregation out of its rut. This is almost always a bad idea, like putting high-test gasoline into a Model T. It just wasn't built for that. Generally speaking, the spiritual pulse of the Frost Heaves Community Church is somewhere between "drowsy" and "coma." And you know what they say about sleeping dogs.

But Pastor read an article in *Today's Pastor* magazine about a church in Wisconsin that conducted a special kind of Ash Wednesday service, and he decided to try it. I could have told him that just because something works in a foreign country like Wisconsin don't mean it'll work in Frost Heaves. But folks have to learn things for themselves.

When Ash Wednesday rolled around, we were all surprised to open the bulletin and find a checklist of sins in it—nothing spectacular, just your basic trespasses like lying, stealing, greed, and so on. Needless to say, this was like going to a vegetarian restaurant and opening the menu to see pork chops, steak, and chicken livers listed.

Pastor Woodstead explained that we were supposed to check off our personal sins. The list didn't include any of your fancier sins, although there was a space for "Other" if folks wanted to get more specific. Right away everyone started to get nervous, until Pastor Woodstead explained that no one was going to see the lists; he was going to collect them and then burn them, which would be symbolic of the Lord forgiving our sins and removing them "as far as the east is from the west," as it says in the Book of Psalms.

The sanctuary got real quiet as everyone filled out their sin surveys. Folks were more nervous than they'd been since taking the Iowa State tests back in second grade, hiding their answers from their neighbors and folding their finished papers in halves or quarters, or even further, into tight little lozenges of iniquity. It made you wonder if the amount of folding was proportional to the degree of sin, although it was hard to imagine what Millie Tuttle had to feel so guilty about.

As it happens, the attendance for the Ash Wednesday service was higher than usual. (There had been a rumor that our organist, Sophie Hamilton, might be away, so the men of the congregation had turned out in record numbers.) Pastor Woodstead saw the sorrowful looks on their faces and was glad to see they had come to the Ash Wednesday service with the proper penitent attitude, but really it was just disappointment at seeing Sophie at the organ; they had been expecting Cindi Buxton to fill in, wearing her black miniskirt. When they saw Sophie sitting there, it was a letdown.

Anyway, it took a while to collect all the papers, and Pastor was surprised to see how many there were. He put them into a fancy silver bowl and had to keep pressing them down to keep them from falling out. Then he put the silver bowl inside a big lobster pot he'd brought from home and he lit the papers with the candle from the altar.

Pretty soon, little flames were licking above the rim of the pot, and you could tell folks were relieved that God really had forgiven their sins, and also, that no one else was going to find out about them. After a minute, though, the flames were big orange tongues shooting out of the pot, and Pastor Woodstead began to realize that he may have underestimated the wickedness of his congregation.

Pretty soon the pot was a blazing cauldron of sin, and Pastor decided it was time to put a lid on the object lesson. "Don't want to set off the fire alarm," he joked as he clamped the cover onto the kettle.

"I already turned the alarm off," Walter Dunton called from the back of the church, in a tone of voice indicating he knew enough to keep an eye on the pastor in case he did anything stupid, which he had.

The next part of the ceremony called for putting ashes on the back of everyone's hand in the shape of a cross. After a minute, Pastor Woodstead figured the flames were out and it was okay to continue, so he took the lid off the pot to get at the ashes. That was his second big mistake.

You see, putting the lid on the pot *had* put the flames out, but it had also created a smudge pot. The moment Pastor removed the lid, a thick column of smoke poured out, like

82

something out of the book of Exodus, little bits of blackened transgressions shooting up into the air and drifting down on the congregation. In no time, the sanctuary was filled with a gray film, so thick that the folks on one side of the aisle looked like ghosts to those on the other side.

"This is all your fault," Fred Kimball said, nudging Herb Cullen.

"I wasn't the one who asked for another sheet of paper," Herb replied. There was a lot of that kind of thing going on.

Pastor Woodstead didn't know what to do. Cecil Buxton stepped out the back door of the sanctuary and got some snow to dump into the kettle. The smoke poured out of the sanctuary and Beatrice Thompkins saw it from her kitchen—she wasn't feeling well that night, and besides, she was mad at her sister Mavis and didn't want to run into her, so she'd stayed home—and she called the fire department.

As it happens, the firemen were all down at the station playing cards and they responded to the call in record time, even though Charlie Greene had been holding a straight flush.

The volunteers put out the blaze and cleared the air in just a few minutes. Charlie thought about citing Pastor Woodstead for half a dozen violations of the fire code, but he was feeling guilty because he's a member of the congregation, and probably should have been at the service in the first place. Instead, he wrote up the incident as a "food preparation fire," as if Pastor Woodstead had been whipping up a sin fricassee or Cajun-blackened trespasses.

Later that week, Pastor Woodstead's wife Betty asked him what had become of the silver bowl she'd received for being

Welcome Wagon volunteer of the year. (She had missed the service because she was in Milliwillitockset visiting her mother, whose arthritis was acting up.) He mumbled something about not knowing, which wasn't exactly bearing false witness. He had taken the bowl to the swap shop at the dump, where it was picked up by Agnes Letourneau. Agnes wondered who would be stupid enough to light a fire in a sterling silver bowl, but figured it would make a good water dish for her cat, Sylvester.

Since Pastor didn't know exactly where the bowl had ended up, he hadn't lied (technically). Of course, if we were to hold another sin barbecue, he'd probably have to own up to that one, but that's not likely to happen. Besides, Betty didn't really care about losing the bowl; it was a bit fancy for her taste, and as I say, folks in Frost Heaves don't really go in for show.

Notes Found on the Church Refrigerator

To whoever keeps moving the silverware: The silverware belongs in the drawer next to the stove, where it is handy when you're cooking. That's where it has always been. "Jesus Christ is the same yesterday and today and forever."
—Hebrews 13:8

To *whomever* wrote that note, the silverware should be next to the sink where it is easier to put away after washing. Just because something has always been done a certain way doesn't mean it's the right way to do it. "Behold, I will do a new thing."
—Isaiah 43:19

That is what's wrong with the church today—people thinking they can take things into their own hands and change them without consideration for anyone else. "The wisdom that comes from heaven is first of all pure; then peace-loving, considerate, submissive . . ."
—James 3:17

What's wrong with the church is people thinking they know better than anyone else and deciding for everyone how things should be run. There's no commandment about where the silverware goes. "Do not add to his words, or he will rebuke you and prove you a liar."
—Proverbs 30:6

Would whoever put the padlock on the silverware drawer please unlock it? I need a spoon for my tea.
—Pastor Woodstead

The Triumph of Beatrice

We recently had a special meeting to vote on a new town motto. The way it came about was like this.

Beatrice Thompkins had been driving past our town sign for thirty years and it had been bugging her for just as long. The town sign read WELCOME TO FROST HEAVES, A FRIENDLY TOWN TO LIVE IN. Beatrice teaches English up to the Vinal T. Holmquist Jr. High School, and she has taught just about everyone who ever lived in Frost Heaves.

Needless to say, that dangling preposition made her dentures itch. "How am I supposed to teach grammar to children who have to pass that sign every day?" she'd say. Finally, she decided to do something about it. "The only thing necessary for evil to triumph is for good men to do nothing," Beatrice said as she aimed her ancient Chevy Cavalier toward the town office. "Daniel Webster."

She pulled into the handicapped space in front of the town office. (Beatrice don't have handicapped plates, but she figured if seniority and having taught most of Frost Heaves's children were not handicaps enough, she didn't know what was.)

Cliff Beaman, who usually works at the town garage, was behind the counter that day, filling in for our town clerk, Edith Wyer, who was out sick. (Edith is sick every third Friday of the

86

month—something to do with unpaid sick days. No one questions it, any more than they would have questioned J. Edgar Hoover about his expense reports.)

Cliff was trying to set the time on his digital watch, poking a bent paper clip into a hole on one side while pressing a button on the other—a task that called for one or two fingers more than he possesses.

"Clifford!" Beatrice said, storming into the office. "How do we go about changing the town motto?"

Cliff slid the pieces of the watch into a drawer as if he were still in seventh grade and she'd caught him drawing pictures of World War II planes strafing each other across his desk. "We got a town motto?"

Beatrice sighed, and Cliff realized he'd fumbled it. Mrs. Thompkins had always made him nervous.

"Do we *have* a town motto, Clifford. And the answer is yes."

He winced. "What is it?"

"I'm not going to repeat it."

Beads of sweat had popped up on Cliff's forehead. This was a pop quiz, and he wasn't prepared, and Mrs. Thompkins didn't give hints.

He stalled. "What's wrong with the motto?"

"To begin with, it is not grammatically correct."

"It ai—isn't?" Cliff said, realizing how close he'd come to the edge.

She glared at him. "No, it is not."

"That's bad."

"Don't patronize me, Clifford. You're not clever enough."

Beatrice blamed herself. Lord only knew how many children had had their education stunted by reading that sign every day. If she'd spoken up sooner, maybe Clifford Beaman wouldn't have turned out to be such a dud.

"I'm sorry, Mrs. Thompkins, but you'll have to check with Edith on that. She'll be in on Monday, and you can—"

"Fine," Beatrice said. "I'll do that."

Bright and early Monday morning, Beatrice stood before Edith Wyer, probably the only person in town who is not afraid of her. Edith told Beatrice that changing the town motto would require the selectmen to call a special meeting. Her tone seemed to suggest there was about as much chance of that happening as there was of the fire department marching naked in the Old Home Days parade.

But Edith hadn't counted on Mrs. Thompkins's thirty years of pent-up grammatical frustration. Immediately, Beatrice got on the horn and harassed the selectmen until they agreed to call the special meeting.

Most folks thought it was the stupidest reason for a special meeting they'd ever heard of, but everyone planned to be there. It was March, after all, and entertainment was in short supply.

The meeting was held at the town hall. Walter Dunton banged the gavel and said, "Let's get started. The purpose of this meeting is to determine whether the town motto should be changed."

Earl Hadley—who is opposed to most things on general principle—jumped right in. "What's wrong with the one we g—"

He stopped, feeling Mrs. Thompkins's eyes on him, and realizing he had wandered into a grammatical dark alley. He backed up and started again. "What's wrong with . . . our current motto?"

"It is grammatically incorrect," Beatrice said. "The correct phrase would be, 'A Friendly Town in which to Live.'"

Charlie Greene muttered, "This is the kind of thing up with which we will not put."

Beatrice scowled at him. Charles Greene had always been a wiseacre, and had not improved with age.

"Who said that?" asked Edith Wyer, who was taking notes for the meeting.

"Winston Churchill," Charlie said.

"What?"

"Never mind," Walter said, and cleared his throat. (Walter has been clearing his throat for thirty years and never manages to dislodge whatever is stuck there.) "Let's get started."

Before the meeting, it was decided that folks would submit their suggestions for new mottoes by secret ballot. (As Yankees, we like secret ballots because it lets you voice your opinion without having to own up to it.)

Walter pulled the first slip out of the ballot box. "Frost Heaves: We'll Grow on You."

Bundy made a lip-fart noise. "Sounds like we're a fungus."

Mrs. Thompkins, who had listened to Nelson Bundworth make farting noises throughout eighth grade, glared at him across the aisle. "As *if* we *were* a fungus, Nelson."

Bundy shrugged, but his cheeks turned pink. Mrs. Thompkins is the one person in town who can call Bundy by his real name.

Walter pulled another slip. "There's No Place like Frost Heaves."

"Ain't that the truth," someone muttered.

The next suggestion was, "Welcome to Historic Frost Heaves." Most folks agreed that this one had a classy ring to it, but we couldn't think of anything historic that had ever happened in Frost Heaves, except maybe the time George Washington passed through town and almost stayed at the Peabody Inn. (I told you about the plaque at the Inn that says, "George Washington almost slept here," which Herb Cullen suggested could also be the town motto, but that got voted down.)

Another suggestion along the historic line was "Welcome to Frost Heaves, Birthplace of—," and the rest was blank. Apparently, whoever suggested that one couldn't think of anyone famous enough to rate putting on a sign.

Walter suggested Philbert Twitcham, our Civil War hero, but we decided that having a historical marker commemorating Philbert's "achievement" was probably sufficient.

Walter moved on. "Frost Heaves—Just a Hop, Skip, and a Bump Away."

"Brings a lump to my throat, that does," Charlie Greene said.

Next came, "Come Get the Cold Shoulder in Frost Heaves."

"Get it?" Roger Coffin said, "Cold shoulder?," so everyone knew it was his idea.

"Welcome to Frost Heaves," Walter read. "Gateway to New Hampshire."

"How can it be the gateway?" Fred Kimball said. "We're in the middle of nowhere."

90

Along the same lines was "Frost Heaves—the Heart of New Hampshire."

"Got the anatomy wrong," Bundy muttered. "It's more like the—"

Beatrice Thompkins shot him an evil glance and shut him up before he could finish.

A few of the mottoes came from the wishful-thinking school of sloganeering: "Frost Heaves Spells Success!"

"That person must have gone to school here," Charlie Dingle said.

"Frost Heaves: A Small Town with a Big Heart."

A few of the ladies went *Awww*, but others worried that this motto might send the wrong message.

"Look," Milt Hazelton said, "we don't want a bunch of shiftless, lazy people who are down on their luck coming here, looking for help."

"Besides," Bundy said, "that describes half the population of Frost Heaves already."

Several suggestions came from the pop school of slogan writing: "Frost Heaves—Watch Us Grow Now." Others sounded like they were written by Barry Manilow: "You've Got a Friend in Frost Heaves."

"What makes you think so?" Earl barked.

There were nostalgic slogans: "Frost Heaves: An Old-Fashioned Town with New Ideas."

"I could use an Old-Fashioned right now," Herb Cullen muttered.

And, of course, there were the purely smart-aleck entries: "Frost Heaves: Write If You Get Work," and "Frost Heaves: Not as Bad as You've Heard."

At this point, Charlie Greene stood up. "Why stop at a motto? I think we need a town song, too. And a town poem." He put one hand on his chest and gazed off toward a corner of the ceiling. "Frost Heaves, my Frost Heaves, thine bumps are home to me . . ."

Walter Dunton had had enough. "It's time to vote. Show of hands," he said, before anyone could call for another secret ballot.

In the end, none of the suggestions got enough votes, so we ended up sticking with the old slogan by default—which is the way most of our town officials stay in office year after year.

Beatrice Thompkins was fit to be tied, but she didn't say anything. The people had spoken, dithered, waffled, and bickered, but she wasn't giving up. She had given the democratic process a try, but now she was going to take matters into her own hands.

A couple days later, Jeff Lamott—he's our other policeman, beside Chief Spaulding—was heading back to town from the speed trap out by the highway when he saw Beatrice Thompkins's old Chevy Cavalier parked by the side of the road. He pulled up behind it, lights flashing, ready to offer assistance.

But Beatrice wasn't in the car. She was heading for the "Welcome to Frost Heaves" sign with an ax slung over her shoulder.

"Mrs. Thompkins," he yelled. "What are you doing?"

"Civil disobedience," she said. "Don't try to stop me, David."

Beatrice took a ballplayer's stance, hoisted the ax off her shoulder, and took aim at that old sign. This put Jeff Lamott in an ethical pickle that would have baffled the ancient philosophers. He couldn't very well arrest his old schoolteacher for vandalism; she was at least partly responsible for implanting in him a sense of duty and responsibility in the first place. On the other hand, he couldn't stand there and let her chop the sign down.

As he pondered this dilemma, Beatrice reared back with the ax. And then the miracle happened. At least, it was a miracle to Beatrice's way of thinking. The wind blew, a high whistling sound that swept through the tops of the spruces along the road. The trees creaked, and loose snow sprinkled down through their limbs.

And the sign started to fall over.

It fell toward Beatrice, who instinctively dropped the ax and held up her hands to keep it from falling on her.

"Oh my gosh!" Jeff Lamott said. He took two steps toward Beatrice as she stood there, holding up the sign, then turned to go back to the cruiser to radio for help. But the chief was off for the day, so who was he going to call? He thought about calling the fire department or the guys at the town garage, but he wasn't sure who was responsible for the sign.

Beatrice yelled, "David, don't just stand there. Do something relevant."

About this time, Charlie Greene came along in his pickup and pulled up behind the cruiser. Jeff trotted over, but before he could say anything, Charlie nodded toward Beatrice, standing spread-eagled against the sign, and said, "I don't know, Jeff. I think you can probably let this one go without frisking her."

"I'm not frisking her, for Pete's sake. She was going to chop the sign down."

Charlie looked at him as if he'd accused Mrs. Thompkins of running a prostitution ring.

"Beatrice?"

"I'm telling you, Charlie—"

"No, I'm telling you, Jeff. This really takes the cake." Charlie liked Jeff, but thought he had a habit of being heavy-handed at times—probably because he'd never made first string on the football team in high school, and still thought he had to make up for it.

"Gentlemen," Beatrice called, but they were too busy arguing to hear her. The sign wasn't really very heavy, but she wasn't going to stand there forever holding it while these two nincompoops decided what to do. "Gentlemen?" They still didn't hear her.

Then the solution came to her, and it was simple in its elegance.

She stepped aside, and the sign fell over with a sickening crunch.

She picked up her ax and strode back to the Cavalier.

"Thank you for your assistance, David."

Jeff Lamott stood there with his mouth open until Charlie said, "Close your mouth, Jeff. Blackflies are out."

So far, we have not replaced the sign. Someone brought it up at Town Meeting, but no one wanted a repeat of the Great Motto Debate, so we did what we always do with difficult issues: nothing. Which is fine with Beatrice, Daniel Webster notwithstanding.

Birth Announcements:

Congratulations to Abner Franklin IV and his wife
Ann on the birth of another daughter, Amelia. Amelia
joins sisters Abigail, Alicia, Amanda, Anna, and Ash-
ley. Abner loves his daughters, but keeps hoping to
produce Abner Franklin V to continue the family name.
With six kids in the roost, we figure Abner has one
more shot at it, as seven is the biblical symbol for
"completion." After that, he better take the hint.

Homer's Oddity

L ately, the church board has been trying to think of ways to modernize things and bring the church into the twenty-first century, or maybe just the twentieth century. Walter Dunton suggested maybe they should take MasterCard in the offering plate, or give out trading stamps. Dave Miller suggested they get one of them satellite TV receivers, so they could beam in a guest preacher every now and then.

Those ideas didn't go over so well with Millie Tuttle. Millie was raised Baptist and tends to be opposed to new technology as a matter of basic principle. (In her younger days, she led an anti-flannelgraph crusade that kept this pernicious device at bay until it was so obsolete that even the Mormons were using it.) These days, Millie goes on about computers and cell phones, and the other board members always hesitate to bring up anything involving new technology, since they know they'll get another long, drawn-out sermon on the subject. One of those every week is plenty.

So the satellite dish was voted down. The only person in town to ever own one of them dishes was Homer Andrews. Homer has the big farm just north of town where the church has its sunrise service every Easter morning. The hardier church members get up early, climb the hill overlooking

Homer's big old barn, and sing "He Arose," with the robins and chickadees singing along as the sun rises over Mount Monadnock in the distance. I tell you, it's enough to make an atheist start to have doubts.

One thing about Homer's hill is that, like a lot of the landscape around here, it makes for great views, but lousy TV reception. Them signals come all the way from Boston or Concord, but when they hit Homer's hill, they just give up. (Generally speaking, the average Third World country gets better TV reception than Frost Heaves. Again, your big cities have got cable TV, but Frost Heaves is likely to get cable about the same time it gets a monorail.)

Homer had been thinking about getting one of those satellite dishes ever since he'd watched the Macy's Thanksgiving Day Parade up close and personal for the first time in his life, at his brother-in-law's house. He mentioned it to his wife Helen a couple of times, but she always came up with something else they could spend the money on. You know how women are.

A few months later, Helen made plans for them to go back to her brother's house over Easter weekend. Homer decided he didn't want to go—said he had too much work to do around the farm. The truth is, he didn't want his brother-in-law rubbing that new satellite system in his face again, bragging about how clear the picture was and how many channels he got.

So Helen went off by herself. Homer spent Friday night twisting the rabbit ears on top of his television, trying to get a clear look at *Francis Goes to the Races*, one of his favorite movies. It was some hopeless.

"That does it," Homer said.

The next day, he called Salerno's Satellite Systems ("A World of Television at Your Fingertips"). Vinnie Salerno come right out in his van to set Homer up with the works—a satellite dish, a new wide-screen television, a digital recorder, and a remote-control device the size of an oak log.

Vinnie surveyed the situation and told Homer the only good place to put the dish would be on top of the barn, on account of the hill being in the way.

"Fine with me," said Homer.

So Vinnie installed the dish and gave Homer the rundown about how it had to be pointed in just the right direction to pick up the signals. He gave Homer a magazine that listed about 120 stations he could get with the system.

Well, Homer was like a kid in a candy store. He watched seven straight hours of television that day. Then he began to feel a little guilty. How was he going to explain this to Helen?

The last time Homer had felt guilty of a high-technology sin was when he was ten years old. He'd snuck off to Keene with a friend to see a movie called *The Ghost Goes West*, starring Robert Donat and Jean Parker. Homer's mother (who belonged to the Millie Tuttle school of theology) found out, and she whipped him good. In her book, movies were the devil's tool for corrupting the minds of innocent youths.

Homer didn't know if his mind had been corrupted or not, but he knew one thing: He'd been in love with Jean Parker ever since that day. He never told anyone, least of all Helen, and he'd never seen the movie again (but he never forgot it).

That night, Homer turned off the TV and was about ready to go to bed, but he couldn't resist taking one more look at the movie guide to see what else was playing that night. That's when he saw it.

At 7:00 a.m. the following morning, one of the movie channels was playing *The Ghost Goes West*, starring Jean Parker. He couldn't believe it; there it was, his favorite movie of all time, starring the woman of his dreams.

Homer set up the machine to record the movie and went to bed, though he could hardly sleep that night, he was so excited. Of course, the other thing that made it hard to sleep was the wind, whipping around the farmhouse. In the spring of the year, the wind can get mighty fierce around Frost Heaves. All night long, the gusts whipped down Mount Monadnock and beat against the sides of the house.

At around 6:30 a.m., Homer couldn't stand the excitement any longer. He got out of bed, turned on the TV, and sat on the couch in his red flannels. (Homer takes off his long johns on May first, the same day he plants his peas.)

Then, at 6:45, right in the middle of the farm news, disaster struck. A blast of wind came down off the mountain like a freight train. The next moment, the picture on the TV screen went from crystal-clear to Siberian-blizzard. Homer jumped up and looked out the window toward the barn. Sure enough, the wind had twisted that satellite dish so it was pointed in the wrong direction.

There was nothing for it but to go out there and straighten the dish, and there wasn't much time. Homer raced to the barn and threw his longest ladder against the side of it, right next to a large pile of fertilizer that he had cleaned out from the barn the day before. He climbed up and made it to the roof.

Fortunately, there was still snow on it, which gave him some traction in getting up the shingles. He reached the peak and managed to get the dish pointed in the right direction with just minutes to spare.

Then he heard it: a sound like a gust of wind bearing down upon him—or maybe like a bunch of people singing—or maybe both.

Then he remembered what day it was.

I'm not sure who was more surprised—Homer, standing on top of his barn roof in his red underwear, or the people coming up the other side of the hill for the Easter sunrise service. At any rate, just as they crested the top of the hill, a mighty wind flew down the side of the mountain. Homer, who had been holding on to the satellite dish, barely had time to take the Lord's name in vain. Then he disappeared, but not before shouting a word that was strangely prophetic, given what was waiting for him down at the far side of the barn.

Later, there was a dispute among the sunrise service worshippers as to what they had seen that morning. Most of them, however, accepted Millie Tuttle's explanation: It was the devil himself, and they had surprised him in the midst of some evil scheme.

Well, they certainly had surprised him.

Anyway, that explains why the church won't be having any satellite dish put in. It also explains the unusual weathervane on top of Homer Andrews's barn. Homer claims it was specially designed according to aerodynamic principles to show the wind direction more accurately than old-fashioned vanes. At least, that's what he told Helen. Folks around here call it Homer's Oddity.

If you'd like to see Homer's weathervane, you should come to the sunrise service sometime. Folks meet at the church before sunrise and come back afterwards for a big pancake breakfast. That's generally the highlight of the service.

But you never can tell.

Police Log: Moose Crossing

Chief Spaulding received a call from Alice Poindexter recently complaining about the moose-crossing sign near her house. "We've had a number of bad accidents there, and I want you to move that sign," Alice said. "There has to be some safer place for them to cross." The chief thought about arguing with her, but decided against it. "You don't argue with Alice when she's got a bug in her sap bucket," he says. So he just thanked her for her suggestion and promised he'd take it up with the town board "real soon now."

Heaves, Hoops, and Earl Hadley

In Frost Heaves, the same people generally run for office every year, so it isn't that interesting. We try to get people excited about the elections, but it's like trying to get a cat to laugh.

One year, we decided that instead of having an election, we would have a talent show, and the winners would get the offices. The problem is, we don't have much in the way of actual talent—unless you count ear-wiggling and the ability to make funny noises with your armpit—so the bar was set pretty low. I'm not going to mention any names, but one of the local ladies, she really wanted to be a library trustee, so she did a belly dance. It weren't a pretty sight. (There's a few of us who still can't get that image out of our heads; it's what you call post-traumatic stress disorder.) Anyway, we give up on the talent election idea after that.

This year, there was some controversy over the position of cemetery trustee. Basically, Mavis and Avis Thompkins (they're sisters) trade off. One year it's Mavis, the next year it's Avis. Well, this year, it was Avis's turn, but Louise Mitchell decided she'd like the job, and threw her hat into the ring. I tell you, it was the biggest controversy to hit this town since they moved the bingo game from the Grange to the town hall. It was a bitter

102

contest, and in the end, Avis edged out Louise. 'Course, Avis had
an advantage, since she and Mavis keep the rolls of all the dead
folks in the cemetery, many of whom actually voted this year.
Edith Wyer was reelected town clerk, of course. And Alfred
Cooper was reelected as supervisor of public works. Basically,
this means he takes care of the town plow. Now, the Frost
Heaves town plow has got about one more year to go before it
qualifies for the National Register of Historic Places. Alfred is
the only person around who knows where to wham it when
the cussed thing breaks down. A delicate piece of machinery
like that, you can't just wham it anywhere; you got to know
the specific location. He'll give it a couple of diagnostic whaps,
and then deliver just the right whack to set it right again.
Kinda like acupuncture.

There were some dirty tricks pulled during the election. I
was helping out with the ballots, and Millard Tuttle came up to
me and told me he would put a dead raccoon in the back of
my truck if Fred Kimball was elected to the board of selectmen. Well, what could I do? I had to report him for attempting
to bribe an election official.

Then, of course, right after election came Town Meeting.
We still do Town Meeting, in contrast to some other towns
around here. We aren't too lazy to do our duty and argue with
our neighbors.

I don't know who first thought of doing Town Meeting in
March, but if you want to guarantee that people are going to
be cranky, just plan a meeting after a long winter. In other
towns around here, people start out with a thin veneer of
politeness, but in Frost Heaves we skip right over that.

The other downside to doing it in March: It conflicts with
the college basketball tournament. Now, we never had a basketball player from Frost Heaves make it to the Final 4 . . . or
the Final 64 (or 1,064, for that matter). But this year, there was
a local boy named Jeremy Russell who plays for Millard Fillmore College over in New York; last weekend was their con-
ference tournament, and there was a chance they were going to
make it to the big show.

This caused quite a dilemma for a lot of the men in town,
who had been watching Jeremy play basketball since he was in
junior high. They had to go to Town Meeting to make sure we
didn't spend a penny more than we had to—but they sure didn't
want to miss that basketball game. Then someone hit on a plan.

Cecil Buxton has one of them old-fashioned hearing aids
that runs to an amplifier in his pocket. He just replaced the
amplifier with a transistor radio, so he could listen to the game
and report to the other guys on the sly. The problem: Although
Cecil knew what was happening at the game, he had only the
vaguest notion of what was happening at Town Meeting.

Which weren't that big a problem, because Town Meeting is
always the same. It's like a play that gets put on once a year. First,
they hand out the town reports. About the only interesting
thing in there is that you can find out who didn't pay their taxes.

The Ladies' Loon League always has a bake sale. This year,
Mabel Pillsbury—she fancies herself the Julia Child of Frost
Heaves—invented a new cake especially for Town Meeting. She
called it Democracy Cake, and it had pineapple, chocolate, arti-
choke hearts, and beef jerky bits. (Generally speaking, I think
democracy is a good thing, but maybe not in food.)

Anyway, the cast of characters at Town Meeting is always the same. First you got Howard Everly; he's the moderator, and follows the rules to a T, always making sure everyone gets a chance to speak. Consequently, getting anything done in Frost Heaves takes longer than it does for fossils to form.

The first item on the agenda every year is the financial report, given by Emmett Tidley, the town treasurer. Emmett loves to give reports—he has, ever since he was a kid in school—and he insists on reading every single line of the report. This is about as much fun as being awake during your own surgery and hearing the doctor describe each step. The only interesting part of the financial report was when Emmett mentioned that receipts for dog licenses had risen 17 percent.

At that point, Cecil Buxton shouted "Whoa!," and folks who had been dozin' off kinda snapped to attention, wondering why he was so excited about dog licenses, but really, it was that the Fillmore Badgers had just taken the lead in the tournament.

After the financial report came the reports from the town committees, most of which I missed because I had had some of Mabel's cake and was experiencing democracy in action, if you catch my drift.

Finally, there were the warrant articles—items that have been put on the agenda so we can vote on them, usually things someone thinks we need to spend money on. This year, you could basically sum up the response to the warrant articles as follows: *No!* Of course, these days, all the towns around here are pinching pennies, but we were cheap long before it become fashionable. In fact, I'm thinking that this recession could actually be good for Frost Heaves. In times like these, people start to focus on the good old-fashioned virtues like honesty, integrity, and common sense. We haven't got any of them, but we do have cheapness. It isn't exactly one of your classical virtues, but it makes a lot of sense.

When it comes to the warrant articles, the same people get up to speak every year. The Town Meeting is their big chance to hold the entire town hostage to their opinions, and they aren't going to miss it.

First you have Clara Franklin, who taught history at the Frost Heaves Academy for thirty years. I say "taught," but for the last ten years, Clara weren't exactly teaching from the book, if you know what I mean. A lot of kids graduated thinking the Gettysburg Address was a place you could send a postcard to. When the school board caught on, they held a quick retirement party for Clara, who looked a little stunned, but managed to lecture her fellow teachers about the Peloponnesian War, the Taft-Hartley Act, and the Gadsden Purchase, without which a southern railroad route to the Pacific would never have been possible, before being drowned out by a chorus of "For She's a Jolly Good Fellow."

These days, when Clara stands up to speak at the Town Meeting, you're never really sure what planet she's broadcasting from. And generally, there is only the flimsiest connection between the warrant article at hand and Clara's comments, which center around a few recurring themes: "The Way Things Used to Be" (better than they are now), "What Young People Need" (discipline), and "Those Idiots Down in Washington."

Clara was going on about the Federal Reserve when Cecil Buxton passed a note to Herb Cullen in the row ahead of him.

Clara saw this and said, "Cecil! Maybe you'd like to share that note with the class." So Herb passed the note to Clara—you don't want to cross Miss Franklin—and she read the note out loud: "Sixty-four to sixty, second half, Badgers lead," and a cheer went up, so Clara decided that was a good time to sit down.

Then Earl Hadley took the microphone. Earl is the town's unofficial contrarian. He is opposed to just about everything, on general principle, because he's kinda cheap. Actually, to say he's kinda cheap is like saying that Hitler was kinda pushy. And every year, he starts off the same way. "My family came to this town in 1790 . . . ," and people start to settle in, 'cause they know they're in for a long haul.

This year the big argument was about whether to buy a portable defibrillator for the fire department. You know what a defibrillator is: It's like a jump-starter for your heart in case all that fried dough you ate at the Eastern States Exposition over the years finally comes to roost in your aorta.

Nobody was too surprised that Earl opposed this idea, which he said was the stupidest waste of taxpayers' money he'd ever heard of. Of course, that's what he says every year, no matter what it is. You'd think the town fathers just sit around all year coming up with a proposal that would top last year's for stupidity.

Well, Earl went on and on. Folks tried to reason with him, but after an hour of arguing about it, they were getting nowhere. The guys from the fire department were pretty fed up; not only was Earl keeping them from getting a piece of equipment they needed, but he was also making them miss the basketball game of the century.

At one point, fire chief Mickey Edwards went off to the bathroom—we all figured he'd had some of Mabel's cake, too—and whilst he was in there, don't you know the fire bell went off. Mickey came running out of the bathroom and yelled, "Come on, men, let's go." And they all jumped up and ran out to do their duty.

Well, it was perfect timing. Someone hollered over to Earl, "You see, that's why we have to support our firefighters and give 'em what they need to do their jobs."

For a moment, it looked as if Earl was going to crumble, but then he shook his head. "I don't care; I ain't voting for it."

By that time, everyone had just about had it with Earl. Someone made an amendment to the warrant, and before Earl could object, it was seconded and passed with a voice vote. And that brought the meeting to a close, to the thunderous applause of the gathered citizenry.

The cheering was so loud that the volunteer firemen heard it all the way over to the fire station, where they were gathered around a satellite hookup to watch the last few minutes of the basketball game. And with just seconds left in the game, Jeremy Russell made an astonishing shot from half-court . . . which bounced off the rim. The Badgers lost by two points, but it's okay. We're from Frost Heaves; we're used to failure.

Oh, and about that warrant article. The way it read, as amended, was: "To see if the town will vote to raise and appropriate the sum of six thousand dollars to purchase a portable defibrillator for use on anybody who needs it—except Earl Hadley."

News Nuggets: New Business on Tap

Local residents Elmer and Homer Cratchet, who always have some scheme going, have opened up a new sugar shack this spring. "We got the idea when we realized we had a nice line of trees right along the road in front of our house," says Homer.

Unfortunately, the trees turned out to be telephone poles. They did get some sap from them, but when you eat the syrup, you get a little shock and your hair stands on end. Makes eating waffles a lot more interesting, let me tell you.

Homer's Spin Cycle

A round here, winter is long and dark, and sometimes even spring seems to be a little depressed, as if to say, "What's the use?" The way some folks deal with this is to buy things to try and cheer themselves up.

Take Homer Andrews. He just bought himself a new rifle. His wife Helen wanted to know why on earth he needed that, and he explained to her that it was an investment. There are a lot of wild turkeys that hang around Homer's farm, and he got it into his head that he was going to fill the freezer with free, organic turkey meat. (If you ever saw the wild turkeys around here, you would know this was not a great idea. These aren't exactly Butterballs, as I think I've mentioned before. They make vultures look positively appealing.)

But Homer's mind was set, so he bought himself that new rifle. Helen, she weren't too pleased. The thing that really frosted her perm was that she had been bugging Homer to buy her a new washing machine for months. Their old machine was on its last legs, and she said it was ruining all their clothes. But Homer said it was still perfectly good, and he wasn't going to waste money on a new machine as long as the old one was still working. So when he bought that new rifle, she gave him a few words about wasting money, and then for a while there was very few words being said. You know how that goes.

The next day Helen was still fuming, and her mood wasn't improved by doing several loads of laundry. We'd finally had a warming spell, so she'd decided to hang the clothes on the line. When that was done, she thought she'd go to town to give herself a chance to cool off a little more.

Homer had finished his chores and was sitting in the kitchen reading the *Frost Heaves Free Shopper,* when out of the corner of his eye he saw a whole flock of turkeys making their way across the yard, passing right under Helen's clothesline.

He quick grabbed his new rifle, but then he hesitated. With the rifle, he would only get off one good shot before the rest of them birds scattered. He really wanted to prove a point with Helen, so he decided to use his shotgun instead, which would maybe let him get a couple of turkeys. He knew this was cheating, but as they say, all's fair in love and domestic arguments.

Homer blasted away, and sure enough, he got three of them birds. He was tickled pink, and by the time Helen came home, he was busy plucking those turkeys. He didn't say much; he was just humming a tune, one that's an old favorite among fighting spouses, the one that goes *Neener, neener, neener.*

Helen didn't say anything either. She just headed out to the backyard to get the clothes off the line. A few minutes later, she came back in with a funny look on her face and said, "You know those brand-new shirts I bought you for Christmas?"

"Ayuh," Homer said.

"Well, that old washing machine has ruined them."

"Really," Homer said. "How so?"

"Look at this," she said. She held up one of the shirts, which had a pattern of holes all through it.

Homer realized pretty quick that the spray pattern of a shotgun was a lot wider than he'd thought it was. Second, he realized that the cost of replacing them shirts was probably going to be more than what he had saved by shooting those turkeys instead of buying 'em at the store. And finally, he estimated the cost to his pride if he admitted to Helen what had actually happened. So he took a deep breath and said, "Well, I guess it's time to get a new washing machine."

"I guess it is," Helen said, and she set to folding the rest of the laundry, not saying another word, just humming quietly to herself: *Neener, neener, neener.*

News Nuggets: Library Exhibit

This week at the library, Millard Tuttle will be displaying items from his large collection of beer cans, including several of his favorites. "They're all Pabst Blue Ribbon cans, so they look pretty much alike," says librarian Mamie Arkett. "But it's still kind of interesting."

A Taste of Honey

It's spring-cleaning time in Frost Heaves. Folks are cleaning up their yards, hauling brush to the dump. Even the kids are getting into the act. Up at the Frost Heaves Academy, the kids are busy cleaning out their minds, forgetting everything the teachers poured into them over the past year so they'll have room for all the characters from their favorite TV show, or the lyrics to songs that'd make your hair stand on end if you still had any.

Eileen Patterson got the urge to clean, and right away found herself overwhelmed. She and her husband Bill have lived in their house for forty years, and as you know, stuff tends to accumulate. (My theory is that there are actually two kinds of stuff, male and female. If you leave the two types of stuff alone in a dark place, like an attic or a closet, they actually reproduce. That's why you open the closet and say, "Where did all this stuff come from?")

Anyway, Eileen took a few things to the swap shop at the dump and got to talking to Louise Mitchell, who, in between being the town lunch lady and the News Nuggets reporter, is also the volunteer caretaker of the swap shop. (Louise likes to call herself the swap shop *docent*, which is a fancy European word meaning "person who stands there and makes sure you're really going to use this and not just sell it on eBay.")

113

Eileen said to Louise, "You going to be here next week?"

"You new in town?" Louise said. "I'm here every week."

"Good," Eileen said. "Because next week, I'm bringing a lot of stuff. We are downsizing." (For you men, *downsizing* means that all your stuff will be out the door before you can say "highly collectible heirloom.")

Frost Heaves is a small town, and you know how it is in a small town (or maybe you don't). Within two hours, everybody knew what was up with the Pattersons. Of course, accuracy isn't exactly a highly prized commodity around here, and the way the grapevine had it, Bill and Eileen were moving to a condo in Florida, and they were taking all their stuff to the swap shop because Eileen had inherited a lot of money from a rich old uncle named Don Sizeman, or an aunt named Donna Seissen, depending on who you talked to.

Anyway, everyone in town was planning to be up at the swap shop come Saturday morning, because Bill and Eileen had a lot of good stuff, and as Yankees, you can never have enough stuff.

Bertha Eldridge, she was real excited about this event, because she had her eye on a solid maple drying rack of Eileen's. But Bertha had a problem. She didn't really want to face Louise Mitchell. She and Louise had not been speaking to each other ever since the great Snowflake Fair Incident. Bertha had outmaneuvered Louise to take over the fair, and although Louise had managed to regain control, the two had been on the outs ever since. Nonetheless, Bertha really wanted to be there when Eileen dropped off her stuff, so she figured she would just have to tough it out.

Most folks didn't feel comfortable showing up to the swap shop empty-handed just to look over Bill and Eileen's stuff, so they looked around for something they could bring to the swap shop themselves, kind of like an admission ticket.

Abner Franklin—this is Abner Franklin III, who just became a grandpa again—he went up to his attic to see what he could find to part with. While he was up there, he came upon his old record player and all his albums, including an old Herb Alpert record that had been a favorite when he was younger. It was called *Whipped Cream & Other Delights*. That's the one with the cover showing a young lady wearing a dress made of whipped cream (and apparently not much else; an awful lot of teenage male fantasies revolved around that album cover).

Abner put on that old record and cranked up the volume—his hearing isn't what it used to be—and it brought back a lot of good memories.

As it happens, while Abner was up in the attic, a bear came out of the woods behind his house, looking for something to eat. This is a bear that has been around town for some years. Back when he was younger, he had stumbled upon a jar of honey in one of the cabins along the town pond, and once a bear gets a taste of honey, there's nothing can stop 'em from coming back.

Nowadays, this bear is pretty old; the other bears call him Old Toothless. There isn't much to eat in the woods this time of year, so he had wandered into town, looking for easy pickings at bird feeders and such. He had been wandering by Abner's house when he smelled the bacon that Abner had cooked for breakfast that morning, which drew him like a magnet.

As the bear sauntered up to the house, Abner was still up in the attic, playing that record at full volume. Now, most bears won't come near a house that is blaring Herb Alpert music— that's a little tip if you want to keep bears away—but this old bear was mostly deaf, so it didn't bother him.

He pushed open Abner's back door and found his way to the pantry, where he had a fine snack of Ritz crackers, Oreos, chips—all the stuff that bears and old bachelors love to eat.

Meanwhile, in the living room, Abner's dog Buddy—an old, white-faced golden Lab—heard the racket and thought maybe Abner was getting a snack, which meant he might get one, too. He waddled to the kitchen door and there was Old Toothless, standing in front of the pantry, devouring an entire package of Do-si-Dos Girl Scout cookies that Abner had just bought from his granddaughters.

The bear saw Buddy looking at him and chuffed, which was his way of saying, "What?"

Buddy considered the situation for a moment. This was his house, and it was his duty to protect it. Also, he really liked those Do-si-Dos. On the other hand, it was a big old bear, and even dogs understand the relationship between discretion and valor.

So Buddy gave a little *woof*, which was his way of saying, "Never mind," and padded back to the living room.

Up in the attic, the record ended and Abner heard a ruckus down in the kitchen. He assumed it was Buddy, so he came tromping down the stairs, yelling "What the dickens you up to?" Despite his hearing loss, the bear heard Abner coming, so he hightailed it out of there. Abner heard the screen door slam and saw the back end of the bear as it disappeared into the woods.

The kitchen was a mess, but Abner's first concern was Buddy. He called Buddy's name a few times, then went looking for him. He found Buddy asleep at his usual spot on the living-room rug—at least, Abner thought he was asleep. When he came into the room, Buddy opened one eye as if to say, "What?"

"Didn't you hear all that?" Abner said.

Now, one of the advantages of being a dog is that you can pretend you don't know what people are saying. Although in this case, Buddy knew exactly what Abner was saying.

Abner shook his head and set to cleaning up the kitchen. He knew he was going to miss out on all the good stuff at the swap shop, but there was nothing to do for it.

Meanwhile, up to the dump, a fair-size crowd had gathered, each person depositing their token offering and then milling around, pretending like they weren't waiting for the Pattersons to show up with the loot. Eventually, Eileen Patterson pulled up in her Subaru wagon and opened the trunk. She pulled out exactly three boxes, including two boxes of old canning jars from when she and Bill used to keep bees, and a complete collection of Robert Ludlum books. That was all she could talk Bill into parting with.

The other folks stared, bug-eyed, then went milling around anyway. The funny thing was, there was still lots of good stuff to choose from, since everyone who came had brought something. It was like the miracle of the loaves and fishes, only this time it was garden hoes and dishes.

Among the items that showed up was a nice wooden drying rack, which Louise Mitchell pulled aside. (That's about the only perk of being the caretaker of swap shop: first dibs.)

Bertha Eldridge saw that drying rack and she swallowed her pride and said to Louise, "What a nice drying rack."

Louise knew exactly what that meant, and at first she was going to tell Bertha that the rack was already taken. But she didn't really need a drying rack; she already had a perfectly good one. And it *was* spring-cleaning time—time to get rid of old things. Including, maybe, old hatchets.

Louise handed the drying rack to Bertha and said, "You take it. I set it aside just for you."

Off in the woods by the dump, sitting on a little rise and watching all this, was a big old bear. He was just sitting in the warm sun, wondering if there was anything good down there among all that junk, remembering a summer day long ago and the amazing find he had come upon in a cabin by a lake, the memory of which had stuck with him ever since.

Meeting Notes: Frost Heaves Regional Economic Development Council

At the June meeting of FRED, Herb Cullen presented an idea for a new business in town. Herb had recently visited an international-themed restaurant called the International House of Pancakes down in East Overshoe. Apparently, there were people from all over the world there, although he noted, "They all spoke perfectly good English." Herb suggested that Frost Heaves should start a chain of restaurants called International House of Beans. "We already got kidney beans and them little beans," he said. "All we have to do is add black beans and pinto beans and a few more. Who knows? It might catch on." Edith Wyer said that smoking would have to be banned on the premises, for obvious reasons. The idea was voted down, five to one.

Bernice's Big Break

The big news in town is that old Bernice Franklin is going to New York City. This came about because of something that happened last weekend.

Bernice got up early Saturday morning to do her laundry like she does every Saturday. (Most folks around here do their laundry on Mondays, but Bernice always was a bit of a rebel.) When she went to dry the laundry, her old Hotpoint dryer broke down.

There she was with a house full of wet laundry, and it was threatening to rain so she couldn't hang it outside. So she called up the Hotpoint dealer over to Keene. He laughed when Bernice read him the model number—let's just say that model had been around since the McKinley administration—but Bernice gave him what-for, and then he got serious and said he'd send someone out. He asked for her address and Bernice explained she hadn't had a number on her house since the ice storm took out her mailbox.

"You'll have to put a number out so we can find the place," the guy said. So Bernice took a piece of paper, wrote a big "13" on it, and nailed it to the tree in front of the house.

As it happens, one of the local art groups was doing a studio tour that day. That's where they give you a map and you drive around and peek into the artists' studios to see what they're up to. This is supposed to give people exposure to new artists and their work, but it's really just nosiness (though it's officially sanctioned, so it's okay).

Now, two fellows from New York City happened to be in town, visiting a friend at the MacDowell Colony (a place that's like summer camp for artists), and they decided to do the tour. They had a rental car with one of them GPS devices in it, so they figured they'd be all set. Of course, everyone knows a GPS doesn't stand a chance against the back roads around here. We have roads that just sit there snickering, waiting for some poor fool with a GPS to come by.

Needless to say—or almost needless—these guys got lost and wound up in Frost Heaves, which isn't necessarily easy to do. They came out of the woods near Bernice Franklin's house and breathed a sigh of relief because, being city folks, they automatically assumed that if you get lost in the woods, some rural maniac is going to kill you, which is only partly true. They saw the big number in front of Bernice's house and one of them said, "Oh, here we are."

Inside the house, Bernice saw the fancy car pull up and figured it was the repair folks, though she was a little surprised to see two fellows. (She was darned if she was going to pay double for this.) She was also surprised at the way they were dressed, both wearing tight black pants, a tall one in a black T-shirt and a short one in a sport coat, neither one of them carrying anything except for a shoulder bag, and that didn't look as if it would hold much more than a screwdriver.

They came to Bernice's front door and when she answered, they said how glad they were to be there because they'd gotten lost, and Bernice said, "Well, you're here now, so come on in."

Bernice had spread the wet laundry all over the house to dry it as much as she could. There were blouses on every chair and table, skirts covering lamps, sheets hanging from curtain rods. The unmentionables were in the bathroom, of course.

Those two fellows walked in, looked around, and right away started nodding and mumbling to each other.

"Very interesting," the short one said.

"Mmmm," the tall one said.

They walked around the living room and Bernice overheard them whispering things like "Duchamp" and "Rauschenberg" and "Dali." She didn't know who they were talking about, but she thought, "They better not try to bring in more people for this job, because I won't pay for it."

Finally, the short one said to Bernice, "What do you call it?"

She raised one eyebrow, wondering how much training it took to become a Hotpoint repairman these days.

"Laundry."

The two looked at each other and nodded.

"Perfect," the tall one said.

"How long have you been doing this kind of work?" the short one asked.

"Sixty years," Bernice said, wondering why. Were they trying to sell her a new machine? They hadn't even seen the old one yet.

"Do you do your own installations?"

"No, I do not," Bernice said emphatically. If she did have to buy a new dryer, she was darned if she'd install it herself.

They glanced at each other again and the tall one took out a notepad and wrote something down. Bernice thought, "That's right; you write that down, and be sure to tell your bosses."

"You know," the short one said, "I find your work to be strikingly original. Reminiscent of Christo, of course—"

"Of course," the tall one said.

"But with a much more organic, rudimental narrative."

"Absolutely," the tall one said. "And this faux-primitive environment," he added, gesturing around the living room. "Brilliant, just brilliant."

Bernice stared at them, wondering if people who escaped from institutions ever dressed up in fancy clothes just to fool you. "Well, anyway," she said, hoping to steer the wayward conversation in the general direction of her dryer, "I can show you—"

"Oh, I don't think we need to see any more," the short one said, pulling out a business card. He handed her the card, which read:

SOTTISE AND L'ARGENT GALLERY
526 WEST 29TH STREET
NEW YORK, NY 10001
BY APPOINTMENT ONLY.

"We'll be in touch," he said. "I think this would go over very well in our space."

"*Very* well," the tall one said.

After they left, Bernice replayed the conversation and eventually figured out who they were and what they wanted. She called them to try and clear things up, but before she made any headway, Louis—the short one—told her how much money he thought she could make with *Laundry: Form versus Function of Saturated Textiles*. (He said he added the extra words because "Our patrons are well-to-do, but frankly, most of them lack the insight to understand the trenchant irony inherent in your original, one-word title.")

So now Bernice is planning a trip to New York City for the opening of her first art exhibit. The only holdup is that she can't decide what to wear; most of her clothes are in the exhibit, and she's still waiting for the guy from Hotpoint to come fix the dryer.

Notes from the Frost Heaves Community Church Bulletin:

The church will be having its annual dinner next weekend, and Helen Andrews asks that anyone with special seating requests let her know immediately. End seats are at a premium because of all the folks with bad knees who have trouble sitting in the middle, but she does have one or two end spots left for anyone who wants to upgrade. She will also try to seat those with a bad ear or cataracts so they can see or hear their spouses (or not; you decide). Just be sure to tell her, and specify which ear or eye you're talking about. Helen also says she cannot honor requests to seat you with "only Democrats" or "only Republicans," even if that ruins the evening for you. "People are just going to have to grow up and act civil," she says.

Let Us Break Chips Together

It's summer, and we've had quite a few visitors in town. First there was a tour group from Massachusetts that came up with the Pixie Bus Tours. They stayed at the Peabody Inn, and on Sunday morning they all went to the Frost Heaves Community Church.

Then there's the new family in town, the Flemings, and they came to church for the first time too. These days, newcomers at church are as rare as Indian Head pennies.

The Flemings came from Virginia. He's a teacher and she used to be a lawyer, but now she's at home with their kids. We're not exactly sure why they landed in Frost Heaves, but we don't look gift taxpayers in the mouth. Needless to say, these are prime candidates for a church that's desperate for new members.

The Flemings walked in to church on Sunday and sat in the Kimballs' pew. Technically, we don't have assigned pews, but everybody always sits in the same place, so it amounts to the same thing. Nobody said anything, because these were newcomers, and we were all on our best behavior.

Everyone smiled at them, trying to be friendly—not typical behavior for Yankees. From the newcomers' view, it was probably a little creepy—everyone smiling at you but no one saying a word, as if you had wandered into a Stephen King movie.

Hazel Northrup, who was sitting in the same row as the Flemings, picked up the Friendship Pad at the end of the pew. The Friendship Pads are legal pads, one for each pew. The idea is for the first person in the row to sign it and pass it to the next person, who signs it and passes it along. When the pad reaches the end of the row, the last person signs and passes it back. That way, if you don't know someone's name, you can just look at the pad as it goes by.

Pastor Woodstead has never been in favor of the Friendship Pads. As far as he's concerned, it's the perfect Yankee contrivance—a gimmick that allows you to get the scoop on your neighbor without the inconvenience of actually speaking to them. When the deacons first suggested it, Pastor said, "If you see someone you don't know, why don't you just walk up to them and introduce yourself?"

"Sometimes folks forget other people's names," Walter Dunton said. "The Friendship Pads give them a way to find out without being embarrassed."

"And they also help you know if there are newcomers," Herb Cullen added.

None of that washed with Pastor Woodstead, especially the bit about newcomers. It would have been easier for a Black Panther to sneak into a Ku Klux Klan meeting than for a newcomer to show up at the Frost Heaves Community Church without being noticed.

But he didn't fight the Friendship Pads, because he knew what the deacons really wanted was for him to stand up every Sunday and say, "Do we have any visitors this morning?," as if a spotlight wasn't already shining on any unfamiliar faces in the

congregation like deer in the headlights. So he went along
with the Friendship Pads, but after a few weeks they hardly got
used, because everybody knew everybody else anyway.

That morning, Pastor watched Hazel sign the pad and pass
it to Peter Fleming, who looked at it as if it were a pop quiz.
Hazel leaned over and told him to sign it and pass it on. A
short time later, the pad made it back to Hazel, who glanced at
the newcomers' names, nodded to them, and then ignored
them for the rest of the service.

Up at the front of the church, Sophie Hamilton was toiling
away at the prelude. As she finished up, Pastor Woodstead
glanced at the bulletin to see what the special number for the
morning would be. He was hoping for something that would
impress the new folks, but what he saw made him blanch.
Mavis Thompkins was in the batter's box for the special number that morning, and she was already elbowing her way to the
front of the choir, like a general advancing to the field.

To Pastor Woodstead, Mavis's voice sounded like rust being
scraped from a wire. A couple times a year, Mavis conspires with
Sophie to do a special number, and this was one of those Sundays.

Pastor stared at the bulletin as Sophie slowly ground out
the opening chords, an old hymn called "Who Will Suffer with
the Savior?" That morning, the answer was everyone. As Mavis
screeched her way through the first verse, Pastor Woodstead
glanced at the newcomers. They looked like one of those nov-
elty books with split pages that can be flipped to create different characters: Their mouths were smiling, but their eyes
looked worried, as if to say, "Is she all right?"

The song finally ended and everybody smiled and nodded at Mavis. (These are good Christians; they would have smiled and nodded if she had performed "Ode to Joy" by belching out the notes.)

Then came the congregational hymn. Pastor Woodstead said, " 'A Mighty Fortress.' Number 427 in the hymnal." The page numbers are posted on the hymn board behind the altar, but Pastor always announces them too, since it takes the older members of the congregation a while to find them—especially Ben Cunningham, and Pastor knew he was going to need Ben that morning. Ben has a wonderful baritone voice, but he's eighty-nine years old, and like Sophie, he's moving slower every year. He don't usually find the hymn till the rest of the congregation has finished the first couple of verses.

On the other side of the sanctuary there's Eleanor Bartlett, also in her late eighties. I told you about her; she's our random-syllable singer. She forgets the words and doesn't see very well, so she tends to make up words to fill in, which gets confusing if you're standing next to her:

Did we in our and now confide
our light and all is lo-oo-oosing
We're not in only, and our side
is where if God is choosing . . .

By the time the congregation reached the last verse, Ben Cunningham had found the right page and joined in, so at least the hymn ended on a high note.

Next came the Lord's Prayer, and here the challenge was Joe Hoffman. Joe is a German Lutheran, Missouri Synod. These people brook no fooling around, and Joe always treats the Lord's Prayer as if it's the Lord's Sprint—whoever gets to the end first, wins. He starts every line of every creed and prayer before anyone else, including the pastor, so there's always an echo effect, with Joe leading the pack:

We believe in God the Father almighty . . . mighty . . . mighty . . .
Maker of heaven and earth . . . earth . . . earth . . .
And in Jesus Christ his only son . . .son . . . son . . .

Still, they made it through the prayer, and then Pastor Woodstead gave his sermon. It was about how situations in life are like the weather, constantly changing—sometimes bitter cold and then turning warm, causing frost heaves on the road of life—but that variation is also what makes the sap flow in the trees and brings forth the sweetness of life, and so on and so forth. As I say, Pastor Woodstead's sermons aren't intellectual barn burners, but every once in a while, he comes out with something that hits home.

Then it was time for communion. As Pastor handed the plates to the deacons, he realized they'd need more communion wafers to handle the crowd. He motioned to Walter Dunton, the head deacon, and whispered, "We need more wafers."

Walter walked to the back of the sanctuary and found Cecil Buxton, who had just come on the deacon board, and said, "Pastor needs wafers."

As it happens, Cecil's hearing aid needed a new battery, and he thought Walter said, "Esther needs wafers." Esther Fernald is eighty-three and always sits in the first row, smack in front of the pastor. Cecil wasn't sure why Esther needed wafers, but he figured maybe she was diabetic and had to have a snack.

He hustled to the kitchen to see what he could find, but there weren't any wafers or cookies. There weren't even any crackers—just a half bag of spicy taco chips left over from the chili cook-off the youth group had held the night before. Cecil knew taco chips probably weren't to Esther's taste, but he figured in a medical emergency, they'd have to do.

He put a handful of taco chips on a plate, carried them back to the sanctuary, and handed them to Walter. Walter looked at them kind of funny, but before he could say anything, Pastor Woodstead motioned from the front of the sanctuary that they were just about to run out of communion wafers.

Walter walked to the front and handed the plate to Pastor Woodstead, who stared at it for a moment, wondering if it was supposed to be a joke. But the deacons weren't practical-joke kinda guys—at least not in church. And he knew they weren't out of communion wafers, because he'd just ordered a whole case of them.

For a moment, he considered that maybe it was a miracle. Maybe the Lord was telling him to spice things up at Frost Heaves Community Church, to become more diverse and welcoming to Latinos. But there aren't any Latinos in Frost Heaves; the nearest ones are the folks who own that Mexican restaurant over to East Mildew, and the more Pastor thought about it, he was pretty sure they were Filipino anyway.

Then he saw Walter and Cecil having a parley at the back of the sanctuary, Walter whispering fiercely into Cecil's ear, and he realized what had happened. By now, though, it was too late to do anything about it. The ushers were walking to the front, communion plates empty, and they were looking for more wafers. So Pastor took a deep breath and divided the taco chips between the two of them.

As the plates were handed around, the folks from the bus tour looked a little confused, but they each took a taco chip, figuring this was some newfangled theological statement. The plate eventually made it to the new couple, the Flemings, where it stopped. And they just stared at it, wide-eyed.

Pastor Woodstead saw this and thought, "That's that. We won't see them again."

What Pastor didn't know was that the Flemings had been having an argument just before coming to church. Andrea Fleming had been saying she was tired of churches that acted as if Jesus was a white Anglo-Saxon, and for once, she'd like to go to a church that saw the bigger picture. In the course of this discussion, she had said, "You know, Bethlehem is not in New England. What if Jesus had been born in Tijuana?"

Now, staring at those taco chips, Andrea decided it was a sign. God had heard her; he was aware of the big picture, and was at work right there in the little town of Frost Heaves, New Hampshire.

Which is a great relief to us, because we need all the help we can get.

Fred Marple

News Nuggets: Book Club News

This coming Tuesday afternoon, the Ladies' Book Club will be meeting at the library. Right now, they are reading *For the Love of Pete*, which is about a man who gets a Gila monster named Pete as a gift. At first he hates it, then he comes to love it, and eventually it changes his life and teaches him some important lessons. Of course Pete dies in the end; they always do. (I hope that doesn't ruin it, if you haven't already read it.)

"Just because this book has been made into a movie, don't think you can skip reading it," says discussion leader Beatrice Thompkins. She isn't naming names, but says those people may be surprised by some of the discussion questions this time.

Rhonda's Tomatoes

It was a strange summer in Frost Heaves, with more rain than most of us can ever remember—the kind of summer that makes you wish you'd kept the receipt so you could take it back.

The rain was especially hard on the gardeners, like Rhonda LaFleur. Rhonda and her husband Rick own the Bait 'n' Beauty Shoppe on Main Street, and Rhonda has a beautiful garden out behind the shop. Whenever she don't have customers, she goes out back and works in it.

Rhonda is one of these folks who are into the environment. She buys organic food and recycles everything, treats nature with respect, and so on. But this year, she has about had it with the wildlife. The deer, the skunks, the woodchucks; they have all been at her garden mercilessly. She has tried everything to keep 'em away: blood soil, coyote pee, you name it. For a few nights, she even had Rick walk around the perimeter of the garden, peeing. But then the neighbors complained, so he had to stop. It didn't work anyway. The critters were just eating everything—beans, leaves, flowers.

The problem is that Rhonda is also an animal lover. She saw *Bambi* at an early age, and it marked her for life. She has always been willing to put up with a little bit of pilferage—it isn't a big deal to lose a little bit of lettuce—but Rhonda is

132

awful protective of her tomatoes. She grows the best tomatoes in town, and she was bound and determined to keep them for herself. However, it felt as if the critters knew she weren't going to do anything, and they were taking advantage of her good nature, which just made it more annoying.

Rick likes to tease her about this stuff. One day he brought his hunting rifle into the shop and set it in the corner. Rhonda said, "What's that for?"

"That's just in case you change your mind about them animals," Rick said.

Now, aside from the gun and the bait display case, the Bait 'n' Beauty Shoppe looks pretty much like your average beauty salon: a couple of chairs, mirrors, curling irons, and several hundred bottles of All-Natural Clarifying Conditioner Mousse with added carrageenan or whatnot. It's the only salon in town, so most of the women in town get their hair done by Rhonda.

Most of the men go to Bert's Barbershop, as he's the only barber in town. Bert runs an old-fashioned shop with two chairs, big old wood-framed mirrors, and bottles of hair tonic like Gentleman's Choice and Jockey's Friend on the counter.

Bert is a talker. You can always count on him to have a racy story, like the one about the young couple that got married and drove over to Portsmouth for their honeymoon. As they were driving, the man put his hand on his wife's knee, and she said, "Now that we're married, you can go a little farther, you know." So he drove all the way to Biddeford.

That's one of Bert's cleaner jokes.

Bert is in his extremely late seventies, and he's been cutting hair for over fifty years. Over the years, he has cut the hair of just about every man and boy in Frost Heaves, including Hector Twitcham, who had a heart attack right as Bert was shaving the back of his neck. (I don't think it was the shave that did it—although seeing Bert with a razor does put the fear of God into folks, for reasons I'll explain in a moment.)

The rescue folks came in and did cadillac-pullman recuperation on Hector right there in the chair, but it was too late. So Bert just finished the haircut; he figured a man can't get buried with half a haircut, and besides, he has a contract with Fernley Funeral Home to do trims on all the corpses anyway, so he was just saving himself a trip.

Before Bert cuts your hair he always says, "How do you want it?" This, even though he basically only knows one haircut, so it doesn't matter what you say, he just cuts it short all over.

Also, Bert's eyesight is getting worse, and he refuses to get new glasses. Still, he does a fair job, if it's early in the day. The problem is, Bert is known to take a little toot now and then from a bottle he keeps under the counter. By mid-afternoon, he is pretty well lubricated, if you know what I mean. Most of the local guys know that you do not get your hair cut by Bert in the afternoon, unless you want it to look like it was cut with pruning shears and an electric kitchen knife. (In some of the big cities this might be okay—they might even charge you more for it—but not in Frost Heaves.)

What with Bert's age, his eyesight, and the dubious state of his sobriety, some of the men have been thinking about going elsewhere. But it's a small town, and you don't make major changes like that without thinking it over long and hard.

Take Ed Whittle, our postmaster. A few weeks ago Ed's wife was nagging him to get a haircut, but he was putting it off because he couldn't face the thought of being scalped by Bert one more time. Ed has a history of bad haircuts that goes back to childhood, when his father decided he could save money with the E-Z Home Haircut Kit ("A Complete Barbershop in a Box!"). Barbers actually love those kits; they make as much money doing repair jobs as they do on original work. Ed's father may have saved a few bucks, but it was at the expense of Ed's pride, which never really recovered from the monthly humiliation of looking like a tennis ball with the mange.

Anyway, one day Ed was walking his postal route along Main Street when he passed the Bait 'n' Beauty Shoppe and saw the sign that said MEN'S HAIRCUTS. Even stopping and reading that sign, Ed felt guilty. You have to understand that men of a certain generation just aren't comfortable having a woman cutting their hair. (It probably goes back to Sunday school and that whole Samson and Delilah story.)

But Ed looked around and didn't see anyone, so he quick-like ducked into the shop. As it happens, Rhonda was free. She put him in the chair and said, "How would you like your hair cut today?," and Ed could tell she really wanted to know.

Ed mumbled that he just needed a trim, so she started in cutting.

I got to tell you, this was an experience Ed had never had before. To begin with, Rhonda's place smells better than Bert's Barbershop. Maybe it's those prehistoric hair tonics on his counter, or the fact that old men and boys have been coming and going for half a century, but Bert's has kind of a stale smell to it.

Rhonda's place, on the other hand, smells like flowers, fresh fruit, and vanilla extract. Rhonda plays classical music on the stereo, while Bert always has some talk-show guy ranting about the government. Also, Rhonda has a very gentle touch; it's like butterflies fluttering around your head. For Ed, this was another new experience—the only other woman to touch his head in his entire life, besides his mother, was his wife Barbara—and he was really enjoying it.

Of course, he was also feeling guilty about having this good-looking woman touch his head, and he felt as if he was cheating—not on Barbara, but on Bert, though that feeling was fading fast. In fact, he was so relaxed that he started to fall asleep, his head tipping back against Rhonda's chest.

Now, Rhonda is a Buxton. And like all the Buxton girls, she is well-endowed, if you know what I mean. So when Ed put his head back, it landed against Rhonda's . . . let's call 'em "adjustable headrests."

At that moment, Rhonda let out a curse that I will not repeat here, but I can tell you it tended to disparage Ed's ancestry on his mother's side. The next moment, she stepped away from the chair and picked up that rifle sitting in the corner.

In that instant Ed's life passed before him, and what he saw was a long string of bad haircuts, about to end in the world's worst haircut.

The next moment, Rhonda threw open the window, stuck the rifle out, and fired at a woodchuck that she'd seen attacking her prize tomatoes. It turns out that, for a peace lover, Rhonda is a pretty good shot. The next thing that woodchuck knew, he was pawing on Heaven's door, wondering what had hit him.

Ed, on the other hand, was thinking he was about to become the second man in Frost Heaves history to die of a heart attack while having his hair cut. As he caught his breath, Rhonda closed the window, put the gun down, and went back to finish Ed's haircut.

It was a good haircut, too, probably the best Ed ever had. But he has decided to go back to Bert's next time. Sometimes, it's best to stick with what's comfortable and familiar, even if it isn't all that great. That's why most of us still live in Frost Heaves. (Of course, when Ed goes to Bert's, he'll be sure to go first thing in the morning.)

Meanwhile, Rhonda's tomatoes took first prize at the fair this year. We don't get many prizewinners in Frost Heaves, so everyone in town was talking about it. At the Market, Ed Whittle overheard someone say that Rhonda had the best tomatoes in town. He started to look pale and thought maybe he should go home and rest for a bit.

News Nuggets: Town-Wide Yard Sale

The town-wide yard sale is next weekend, and everyone is invited to participate. This year we are making up official signs because of the problem we had last year. It seems that some people from away couldn't tell which houses were participating in the yard sale and which just had their regular junk out front. A lady from Massachusetts offered Millie Tuttle fifty bucks for the old rocking chair on her porch, and Millie would have taken it, except that her husband Millard was asleep in the chair at the time—and he woke up as they were carrying the chair to the lady's car.

Why Bundy Hates Vacations

Every August, Bundy takes a vacation up to the camp, whether he wants to or not. The camp is north of town on Lake Mahoosic (which is actually more of a pond, but folks with water property tend to get some pretentious). Anyway, Bundy's wife Doreen inherited the camp from her folks, the Leonards. Doreen's pa died in '79, and her mother Velma lives by herself on Main Street in town.

Once a year, Doreen and Bundy go up to the camp and spend a couple of weeks there, and Velma comes along, and that's the first reason that Bundy don't particularly like vacations. When he and Doreen are at home and his mother-in-law comes over, Bundy can escape to the cellar and rearrange his jars of perfectly good used nails, or maybe go check his prize long-haired cows. (Fortunately, neither Doreen nor Velma ever asks exactly what he's checking 'em for.) But when they're at the camp, Bundy doesn't have any place to hide—or at least nowhere that Velma can't find him.

Another reason Bundy doesn't like vacations is that he owns the town garage, which he took over from his father, Nelson Sr. (Bundy is Nelson Jr., but as I said before, don't ever call him that to his face if you plan to have work done on your car in this century.) Bundy practically grew up in the garage, so he feels attached to it. The only time he leaves it is the two weeks when he goes to the lake, at Thanksgiving when they go to visit her brother's family in Claremont, and when someone dies.

When he does go away, he leaves Arthur Bascom in charge. I mentioned Arthur to you earlier. When he was a kid, Bundy thought Arthur was a hot ticket. But as Bundy got older, he began to figure out that while Arthur was some handy at fixing cars, he weren't exactly overstocked in the common sense department. (Or, as Bundy says, "His 'check engine light' has been on for a long time.")

Bundy's only other employee is Raymond Kellogg, a town boy who has been in high school since Kennedy took office. Raymond's goal in life is to get *out* of high school. (Actually, I think the folks over to the regional school finally did give him his diploma, on the condition he don't tell nobody where he got it from.)

So as you can imagine, it makes Bundy somewhat nervous to leave his business in his employees' hands. However, Doreen always insists that he take two weeks away from the garage every year, because:

1) "You need a break,"
     and
2) "It's all I ask."

When the wife comes up with arguments like that, you can't say much. So, every year Bundy finds himself at the lake, not knowing what to do with himself without a socket wrench

WELCOME TO FROST HEAVES

in his hand. You can only change the oil in your own car so
many times in a given week.

Bundy does his only leisure reading for the year during
these trips, which is mostly the classics: old *Reader's Digest* Con-
densed Books. The Leonards left enough of those to build a
small house with (which probably wouldn't be the worst use
for them).

Other than that, Bundy spends his two weeks worrying
about the garage and trying to stay out of earshot of Velma.
This isn't exactly easy, since the old lady is a bit more than
somewhat deaf, which means that Doreen has to speak up to
make herself heard, and Velma figures to match her daughter's
decibel level and then some.

This is bad enough when the two of them are just passing
the time of day, but it gets some god-awful when they start
yelling at people to leave the loons alone.

I should explain that Velma and Doreen are members of
the Ladies' Loon League. I think I mentioned that the ladies
have managed to drive away most of the loons, who apparently
decided to find quieter spots for themselves. However, a pair
did come back to Mahoosic last summer, so Velma and Doreen
were in their glory, practicing loon noises and standing in the
pond weeds in front of the cabin, yelling at canoers and kayak-
ers to leave the loons alone.

Generally, the people in the canoes would look indignant
(or as indignant as they could, given that they were in a canoe)
and then take their sweet time paddling away. But one pair of
canoers must have been from New Jersey, because don't you
know, they started yelling *back* at them, if you can imagine.

That only got the ladies more steamed up, especially Velma, who could only imagine what they were saying.

As the paddlers and the Loon Leaguers traded niceties, Bundy opened up the hood of his car, hoping that he looked like a mechanic who had been called out from town and didn't really know these ladies.

Well, the paddlers kept getting closer to where the loons were nesting, and that did it for Doreen. She stomped into the house and rang up the police to complain. She got Jeff Lamott, who was on duty. Jeff told her it wasn't his jurisdiction, which if you knew Jeff wouldn't surprise you; if it isn't a multiple homicide–arson–terrorist threat, he isn't interested. He told Doreen she'd have to call the state game wardens.

Needless to say, talking to Jeff hadn't exactly pacified Doreen any, so she went ahead and called the wardens, except there weren't no answer, so she left a message on the answering machine and went back to her debate with the paddlers.

Eventually, the people in the canoe got tired of the confabulation and took off, but Velma and Doreen managed to keep up their end of the discussion—loud enough for anyone within several miles to hear—about the rudeness of some people, and can you imagine the nerve, and that kind of thing.

Bundy had finally had about enough of this, so he put on his swimming trunks and took off in his own canoe for a paddle. He had got about halfway across the lake when he heard Doreen out in front of the cabin, calling to him. He leaned forward in the canoe and said, "What?"—and accidentally knocked the paddle into the water.

Wouldn't you know, just about then, a motorboat came by, and the wake from the boat sent Bundy and the paddle off in opposite directions. Bundy's direction happened to be right toward where the loons were nesting. He realized this; he just couldn't do too much about it at that point.

Doreen didn't realize what had happened to the paddle. Standing on the shoreline, she instructed Bundy to maintain the proper distance from the nesting waterfowl, only not in those exact words.

Bundy gave Doreen some instructions of his own at this point, which fortunately for their marriage she couldn't hear, as they were drowned out by the approach of a motorboat. This one was driven by a young man in a khaki uniform with a patch that said GAME WARDEN.

Needless to say, Bundy was some surprised, especially when the game warden asked to see some identification. You may remember me saying that Bundy had put on his swimming trunks just before taking out the canoe, so he didn't have any identification on him. (Well, he did, but it was something that nobody else had ever seen besides Doreen, Bundy's mother, and the doctor who had delivered him. Given its location, Bundy didn't think that the warden would especially appreciate seeing it, either.)

Anyway, the warden ended up giving Bundy a ticket for harassing wildlife. Cost him $50. Needless to say, the boys at the Blue Bell Diner have gotten a lot of mileage out of that one. But not when Bundy's around, of course; you never know when you might need to get your car fixed in a hurry.

News Nuggets: New Scenic Drive

The state highway department had a load of asphalt left over from a job recently and asked if we wanted it. The men from the town garage told them to put it on Scoopnagle Road, which has been looking run-down. Unfortunately, they put it on Old Scoopnagle Road, which as you may know ends just past Bernice Franklin's house, although you could travel it if you were crazy or from away and didn't know any better.

At any rate, they paved it, and now Old Scoopnagle Road is the nicest road in Frost Heaves, even if it does end in the middle of the woods. So the guys at the town garage have put up a sign that says SCENIC DRIVE.

"The road goes right past Chester Franklin's pig farm, which makes it an aromatic drive as well," says Bill Patterson, town road agent. "And when you get to the end, you have to turn around and drive past the farm again, only this time you know what's waiting for you. It's kinda like deciding to have a second child."

143

The Town Cane

There was a funeral last week for Wilbur Stonebridge. Wilbur hadn't actually lived in Frost Heaves that long. He used to live in Albany, but when his wife passed away, his daughter Diane asked him to move in with them. Wilbur told her, "I would rather die than live in Frost Heaves."

Wilbur was not the first person to say that, but when you are getting on in years, you have to be more careful. He arrived here in February just in time for his ninety-seventh birthday. That week, the selectmen showed up at Diane's house and awarded him the Ebenezer Tinkham Cane, which is always held by the oldest resident in town. (A lot of towns in New England have the Boston Post Cane, donated by the *Boston Post* newspaper back in 1909. We had one, but it was broken by one of the recipients a while ago. Actually, it was the wife of the recipient, who broke it over the head of the recipient, during an argument about toilet seats. Someone had an old cane that belonged to Ebenezer Tinkham, so that's what we use now.)

Anyway, they gave the cane to Wilbur, and six months later he was gone. The funeral was quite nice, although it was a bit long, thanks to our organist Sophie Hamilton. I think I've told you about Sophie; she has three speeds: slow, slower, and "The pot roast will be charcoal by the time we get home."

We did think about asking Frank Webber to play at the funeral, but as you may recall, Frank only knows Broadway show tunes, and somehow "Put on a Happy Face" and "Everything's Coming Up Roses" didn't seem appropriate at a funeral.

After Wilbur passed away, the selectmen brought the cane to Enid Russell, the next-oldest person in town. Enid met them at the door holding a shotgun and told them in highly colorful language what they could do with the cane. Enid's feeling is that as soon as you get the cane, people start waiting for you to die, and she is not ready to hand in her bingo card just yet, thank you.

Actually, a lot of the older folks in town are superstitious about the cane. The only person in town who really would like the cane is Millie Tuttle. Millie is seventy-two, and she has never had her name in the newspaper in her entire life. There was that time a while back when everyone thought she was lost in the ice storm, but even then the paper just called her "an elderly resident." They were trying not to embarrass her, but she wished they had used her name. In Frost Heaves, most folks are proud when they are mentioned in the newspaper, even if it's just the police report.

At seventy-two, Millie figures her chances of ending up in the police report are pretty slim, and the only other way she's going to make it into the newspaper is by getting the town cane. The problem is that several people are ahead of her in line to get the cane.

After Enid turned it down, there was a fair bit of discussion about who would get the cane next. First, there's always the problem of determining when folks were actually born. As you may have gathered, truth is another commodity that is not overly valued in Frost Heaves, and that goes for birthdays, too. And as I say, the idea of being awarded the cane makes folks nervous.

At any rate, everyone has been talking about the matter of the cane, especially the seniors. Most of 'em were at the monthly supper at the church that weekend. (As I've mentioned, for these seniors, the monthly supper is pretty much the sum total of their social life. They are always there when the door opens, like wobbly racehorses at the starting gate.)

The Frost Heaves Community Church does not have a big kitchen, so the way the suppers work is, the ladies all cook at home and then bring the food to the church. This weekend was a meatloaf dinner, and Millie Tuttle was mixing up her special recipe when she realized she didn't have any mushrooms. She sent Millard to the Market to buy some, but all they had was the organic kind, which cost $5 for a little box. Millard was darned if he was going to pay $5 for a box of mushrooms when he had a backyard full of mushrooms at home, thanks to all the rain we've been having. So he went home, found an old blueberry box in the garage, picked a few mushrooms, and gave 'em to Millie.

Millie finished making her meatloaf and took it up to the church. When she got home, she was cleaning up and she noticed that the bottom of the mushroom box was stamped BUXTON'S BLUEBERRIES. Millie put two and two together and she went looking for Millard, who had wisely vacated the premises. Then she started to panic, because she was pretty sure those mushrooms in the backyard were poisonous.

She raced up to the church, where they had just started serving the seniors. The only non-seniors there were Martin and Sarah Kessler, who had heard the church was having meat-loaf and were pretty excited. They have loved Meat Loaf ever since they were in college, and were really looking forward to hearing him sing "Paradise by the Dashboard Light."

Millie arrived at the church, not knowing what she was going to do. Once you put a meatloaf on a serving platter, it's pretty hard to tell it from any other meatloaf. She raced into the vestry, and there were all the seniors, sitting down and getting ready to be served.

Millie hesitated for just a moment. It occurred to her that most of the people who were ahead of her in line for the town cane were in that room. If she kept her mouth shut, she could wipe out all the competition in one fell swoop. Not only would she get the cane, but she'd probably even get her picture in the paper.

She only hesitated for a moment, though, because she is a good Christian lady, and would never cause anyone needless suffering. Not to mention that her reputation as a cook would really hit rock bottom. Even in Frost Heaves, people tend to remember when your cooking kills more than one or two people at a time.

So just as the church ladies began serving the meatloaf, Millie shouted, "Don't!"

Everybody stopped what they were doing, including Helen Andrews, who was just walking out of the kitchen with a meatloaf pan that Millie would have recognized a mile away.

Everyone looked at Millie, who hesitated for a moment, then said, "Don't . . . forget to say grace." She looked around and pointed to Cecil Buxton. "Cecil?"

When it comes to long-winded prayers, Cecil is the record holder. Buildings have become eligible for the National Register of Historic Places in less time than it takes for Cecil to say grace, and Millie knew that.

While Cecil prayed, Helen Andrews set the meatloaf down on the serving table and closed her eyes. By the time she opened her eyes the meatloaf had disappeared. For a moment, she wondered if there had been some kind of miracle—the Ascension of the Meatloaf or some such. But then she just chalked it up to a senior moment and went back to the kitchen to get another meatloaf.

Meanwhile, Millie drove home to dispose of the toxic loaf. She was going about sixty when she passed Chief Spaulding, who was falling asleep in the squad car out on the highway, where he was hoping to enhance the town's revenue with the help of some out-of-staters. But it was a slow evening and he was drowsy, listening to an old rock song on the radio about a guy on a motorcycle when Millie Tuttle sped past.

The chief pulled Millie over and said, "Mrs. Tuttle, where you going like a bat out of—"

Millie shot him a look. She had been his Sunday school teacher when he was a kid, and she wasn't about to tolerate bad language from him, even if she was on the lam for assault with a deadly meatloaf.

"Mrs. Tuttle, I'm afraid I'm going to have to write you up," the chief said.

Millie thought for a moment and said, "Will my name be in the paper?"

News Nuggets: Meat Raffle

Next Saturday, the men of the Loon Lodge will hold
their annual summer meat raffle, with an interesting
twist. The price of meat has been so high lately that
they decided to have a roadkill raffle instead. They
have been collecting prime specimens and throwing
them in the freezer all year, and have accumulated a
very nice selection. Don't miss the excitement and
the mystery, next weekend at the Grange Hall.

Saying Good-Bye

This coming Tuesday, Dave Miller from the FRED council will be giving a talk at the town hall called "Blogging for Beginners." As you know, Dave is our resident technology nut, and blogging is like keeping an online journal. All kinds of folks are doing it. The beauty of blogs is that, instead of sitting at the local diner and listening to people spout off on subjects they don't know the first thing about, you can sit in the comfort of your own home and do it. Makes it much easier to ignore them that way.

We're expecting a good turnout for Dave's talk. Not because of the topic; most folks in Frost Heaves don't know the first thing about computers, and couldn't care less. They just come for the refreshments. But we are hoping to cheer Dave up. He's been in a funk lately, ever since his old car died. It was a 1987 Buick Century, a big car with a color that's hard to describe—kind of a greenish brown, like the hairballs the cat coughs up.

But it was Dave's first car, and he loved it. He got it right out of high school, bought it with his own money. His father Gordon told him it was a piece of junk and he was wasting his money. You know, nothing inspires a young person like that kind of encouragement from the old man. So Dave was bound and determined to keep that car running, and he did. Over the years, he replaced just about every part you can replace in a car. And then, the last few years, it began to develop some eccentricities.

To begin with, the only way to start the car was to put the key in the ignition and hit it with a hammer before turning it. So he kept a hammer in the car at all times, and didn't worry too much about anyone trying to steal it.

Also, the gas gauge died, so Dave would write the odometer reading on the dashboard with a piece of chalk every time he filled up. Then when he had gone about 300 miles or so, he knew it was time to fill up again. As long as he had a fresh piece of chalk he was okay.

The front passenger-side window wouldn't roll down. Stepping on the brakes was mostly an act of faith. And over the years, he had replaced most of the metal in the body with Bondo, which is like industrial-strength pancake makeup for your car. (That old Buick had so much Bondo on it that Dave always felt a little guilty when he pulled up to a gas pump that said WARNING: DISPENSE INTO APPROVED METAL CONTAINERS ONLY.)

Of course, all this drove his wife Marie crazy. She had been after him for years to trade the Buick in. "Just because it's called a Century doesn't mean you have to keep it for a hundred years," she'd say. But he always said there was nothing wrong with it, and just kept it running.

The thing is, that car held a lot of memories for Dave. He took Marie on their first date in that car, and quite a few dates after that, including most of the movies shown at the drive-in theater over to East Mildew during their junior and senior years of high school. Of course, I'm not sure they could tell you the details of any of those movies, if you catch my drift.

They went on their honeymoon in that Buick, and when their kids were born, each one of 'em came home in it. They went on family vacations in it, and when Dave's father was diagnosed with lung cancer, Dave drove him to his doctor's appointments in it, both of them wondering whether his father or the Buick would last longer. The Buick won.

Still, there comes a time when you've done all you can and you just can't do any more. Dave's birthday is this month, and the inspection was due, so he brought the car to Bundy's garage for its annual physical. Bundy doesn't have one of them fancy computers to fix cars with. He has a screwdriver. He goes around, tapping with the screwdriver, listening. He gave the Buick the once-over, and then he looked at Dave and shook his head.

"What?" Dave said.

"It's time," Bundy said.

"What are you talking about?"

"It's time," Bundy said, and then Dave knew Bundy wasn't going to give him a sticker this time. And if Bundy wouldn't put a sticker on it, that was the end of the line.

Dave was ticked-off. He just stormed out, didn't even take the car. Bundy didn't mind; he just moved it around the back. He's got a lot of cars back there. They aren't really there to be repaired. It's more like a hospice for cars. Sometimes Bundy imagines them back there at night, trading stories about the old days when cars were big, the roads were wide open, and gasoline was 30 cents a gallon.

Dave went home and told Marie the news. She gave him a big hug and told him how sorry she was, but inside she was singing "Happy Days Are Here Again." She was already trying to decide between a minivan and a four-wheel-drive station wagon.

They ended up with a minivan. A few days later, Dave stopped by Bundy's to clean out the old Buick. Bundy thought about offering to help him, but he knew there are some things a man has to do by himself.

Dave headed out back and Bundy finished changing the oil in Walter Dunton's Subaru. When Walter stopped by to get his car, he looked out the back window and said to Bundy, "You see this?"

There was Dave, standing there with his back to them. He was holding a bag of junk—old maps, toys his kids had lost between the seats, brochures from vacation spots, a cassette that he and Marie used to listen to on the way to the drive-in. It looked as if he was talking to that old car, and every once in a while, his shoulders would shake a little.

"What the heck is he doing?" Walter asked.

"Saying good-bye," Bundy said. "Just saying good-bye."

Backword

If you skipped the foreword to this book, you may be wondering what this section is about. In that case, you should probably go back and read it first. Go ahead, I'll wait.

Are you back? All right, then. I know I pooh-poohed the idea of a backword back in the foreword, but now that we've come to the end of this volume, it doesn't seem like such a bad idea after all. Who knows; maybe it will catch on.

At any rate, I'm not sure I've accomplished what I set out to do, which was to tell you a little about our town and maybe contribute a skosh to the effort to put Frost Heaves back on the map. That's probably a futile enterprise—not the first we've undertaken, as the evidence will show.

But we Yankees are nothing if not persistent, or maybe *stubborn* is a better word. So we'll keep at it, if only because we've learned that failure is not the worst thing that could happen, and may actually turn out to be a good thing in the end. It's like the heaves in the road I talked about. If you fight 'em, you just end up with a sore butt and a kink in your neck. But if you take 'em in stride, it can actually be a fun ride.

Well, that's it. I've got a lot more to say about Frost Heaves, but I'll have to get to that another time. I'm not going to hang around, hemming and hawing like those folks who stand at the door and can't seem to say good night, no matter how much you stretch and yawn. I can take a hint.

Thank you for your attention.

About the Author

Fred Marple is often confused with author and humorist Ken Sheldon, a lifelong New Englander who grew up living in old houses, eating baked beans, playing bingo, and picking blueberries. His writings have appeared in a wide variety of publications, including *Yankee* magazine, *The Old Farmer's Almanac,* and *New Hampshire* magazine.

An accomplished performer, Ken made his dramatic debut in a way-way-off-Broadway production of *Mr. Grumpy's Toy Shop* at the Albertus W. Becker School. (He played the lead, a demanding role that required him to remain onstage for minutes at a time, remember several lines, and not sing, ever.)

Ken is the creator of the live variety show *Frost Heaves,* which has been called "hilarious," "outstanding," and "much more professional than I thought it would be."

About the Show

Frost Heaves is a variety show of Yankee music, comedy, and nonsense presented by The Frost Heaves Players who celebrate all that is wacky and wonderful about New England, led by Fred Marple. Winner of a "Best of NH" award, Frost Heaves has been called "Hilarious," "Outstanding," and "more fun than the time Elmer Cratchet put the live lobster in the punch bowl at the church supper.